simply allergy-free

Quick and Tasty Recipes for Every Night of the Week

Elizabeth Gordon

PHOTOGRAPHS BY MELANI BAUMAN AND LORNA PALMER

LYONS PRESS
Guilford, Connecticut

An imprint of Globe Pequot Press

Lyons Press is an imprint of Globe Pequot Press.

Project editor: Meredith Dias
Text design: Sheryl P. Kober
Layout artist: Maggie Peterson

Library of Congress Cataloging-in-Publication Data

Gordon, Elizabeth, 1976-

Simply allergy-free : quick and tasty recipes for every night of the
week / Elizabeth Gordon ; photographs by Melani Bauman and Lorna Palmer.
page cm
ISBN 978-0-7627-8618-3
1. Food allergy—Diet therapy—Recipes. I. Title.
RC588.D53G673 2013
641.5'6318—dc23
2012044119

Printed in the United States of America

10 9 8 7 6 5 4 3 2 1

{ For my mother,
who showed me that nothing is impossible. }

Contents

Introduction

When I sat down to write this book, I asked myself what I wanted to accomplish this time around. With my first book, I wanted to show my readers that they could be terrific bakers despite multiple food allergies. In my second book, I set out to create recipes that were evocative of happy times, times spent with family and friends; I wanted to share familiar recipes that could be passed down through the generations, recipes that transcended food allergies and tasted delicious. But with this book, I want to invite you, dear reader, into my kitchen and give you access to the dishes that I really cook every single day. I want to show you that my food allergies are not a hindrance; they are a lifestyle. My food allergies do not make my life expensive or labor-intensive.

Long before I wrote cookbooks, I was just a girl in Ohio. My mother cooked for us every night, and though I know that this sounds very Norman Rockwell, in fact, it was quite pragmatic. Yes, of course, we sat down as a family every night and talked about our days, but really these family dinners were about making food that was budget conscious, quick, and healthy. Today, I cook dinner for my family as many nights a week as I possibly can. It's less expensive and safer for me to eat this way, because there is little risk for an allergic reaction when I know all the ingredients in my food. Thanks to work, school, extracurricular activities, and life in general, this scenario isn't always realistic for every family, every night, but I still believe in cooking dinner as often as possible. You will see that many of the recipes in this book are freezer friendly and can be made ahead of time so that you can get dinner on the table lickety-split. There are several slow-cooker recipes in this book, because I found that using the slow cooker lets me out of the kitchen to spend a few extra minutes with my children and to enjoy all of the other aspects of my life.

To me, life is about wonderful celebrations, family, and friends, but it is also about daily living and living each day to the fullest. I like to make things that are interesting, colorful, wheat- and egg-free for me, and that I could just as likely serve on a Tuesday night as on Thanksgiving. I do not like to make fussy or expensive things, just straightforward, practical, delicious food that doesn't cost a fortune to prepare. It's important to me that these recipes can be mixed and matched to form fantastic menus and that the leftovers from tonight's dinner could be reworked just a little to make something delicious tomorrow night. I like to think of these recipes as the little black dress of my pantry—simple and economical fare that can be dressed up or down depending on the occasion. The foundations of a great meal, these are recipes that never go out of style.

To me, beauty and adventure are also important to daily living, and I like my recipes to reflect both. Eating is just as much a visual experience as it is about flavors and textures, so I try to create colorful recipes that not only taste delicious but also look appealing. Variety is also important from both a taste and health perspective. No one, not even our taste buds, likes being bored, and I truly believe that multiple food allergies should never translate into bland food. Hence, you will find many different ethnic foods within these pages.

I hope that you will find *Simply Allergy-Free* the definitive book on quick and easy gluten-, dairy-, soy-, nut-, and egg-free daily dining. The recipes inside are delicious and beautiful, things you will want to serve again and again, dishes for weeknights and special occasions alike. From Apple Streusel Cake (p. 138) to Zucchini Fritters (p. 110), I hope that you will enjoy this peek into my gluten-, dairy-, soy-, nut-, and egg-free recipe box. This is how my family eats every day of the year, and I hope yours will, too.

A Brand-New List of Ingredients Defined

Cooking and baking your way around multiple food allergies sounds hard, but it's a snap once you get the hang of it. The first thing you will need is a shopping list and an explanation of some of the new ingredients you'll need to stock your pantry and freezer. Perhaps you've never heard of these ingredients, or maybe you have some of them on hand already; either way, we are so lucky that many of these items have become commonplace in today's supermarket. This wasn't the case when I was diagnosed with food allergies. If you cannot find a couple of these ingredients in your local market, don't worry: Most stores will happily order items for you, and if that doesn't work, Amazon carries almost all of them. Check the Where to Shop section at the back of this book (p. 182) to find alternate places to buy all the ingredients you will need to get started.

Agave Nectar—By now you surely have heard of agave nectar. I see it on almost every supermarket shelf now that Domino Sugar is bottling it. Agave comes from a cactus and has a lower glycemic index than, say, sugar or honey. But that's not why I use it. I use it in icebox pie-crust recipes because it imparts neutral flavor and helps hold the crust together. Plus it is sweet and delicious.

Baking Powder—Baking powder is a leavening agent that is used in larger amounts than baking soda, and it does not need to be activated with an acid. Make sure to check that your baking powder is gluten-free. Not every brand is; be leery of brands made with modified food starch because that is another term for wheat starch. Brands made with corn or potato starch are safe.

Chile de Árbol—*Chile de árbol* is a thin, red, Mexican chile pepper that I usually buy dried in packets. I use this to give heat to dishes like my Chicken Posole (p. 14). Just a little goes a very long way and will liven up any dish that needs zip.

Chinese or Superfine Rice Flour—I used to avoid rice flour at all costs because, unless it is ground superfine, it tends to make recipes sandy and coarse. However, a friend recommended that I try superfine rice flour a few years ago, and I was sold. At first I bought it at the Chinese bodega, but then I found Authentic Foods' Superfine White Rice Flour online and have never looked back. It is flavor neutral, which means that the cookie dough tastes great even before it is baked, and the texture is never gritty. When I refer to superfine or Chinese rice flour, I am always referring to the white variety. Superfine brown rice flour weighs more and will change the outcome of your recipe. See the Where to Shop section (p. 182) for brand names and where to purchase them.

Cider Vinegar—I use cider vinegar in my baking recipes to activate the baking soda. In traditional recipes, acidic buttermilk serves this purpose. The good news is that the vinegar is tasteless in the finished product and even in the raw batter.

Coconut Milk—Some of you may be wondering how coconut found its way into this book. Though the US Food and Drug Administration (FDA) reclassified coconut as a tree nut, talking with doctors and researchers on the board of the Food Allergy Research and Education (FARE) convinced me that coconut is actually part of the palm family and that it very rarely causes reactions in people with tree-nut allergies. Of course, I am not a doctor, so please check with yours before you use coconut products in your cooking. I love canned coconut milk because it is nondairy and great in things like curry, where it is desirable to taste the coconut flavor and the dish requires creaminess. If you aren't crazy about coconut flavor, use the other kind of coconut milk, the kind you find in the dairy section that comes in "milk" cartons instead. Also, the solids in canned coconut rise to the top and, when refrigerated, can be whipped into dairy-free Whipped Cream (p. 181)!

Cultured Coconut Milk—Cultured coconut milk is my go-to substitute for traditional buttermilk. I prefer the original flavor, but if you are using it for baking a cake, try the vanilla. It's good, too.

Corn Flour—Corn flour is different than cornmeal, so pay close attention when you are buying it in the supermarket. Corn flour is very finely ground and not as coarse as regular cornmeal. It is available in most supermarkets. If you cannot find it in the baking section, look in the international section with the salsa and taco fixings.

Dairy- and Soy-Free Margarine—Earth Balance dairy- and soy-free margarine is, in my opinion, the best tasting butter stand-in on the market. I usually prefer solid, organic palm fruit oil shortening (it now comes in dairy-free butter flavor, too) for baking, but Earth Balance is great for spreading or for making, say, a risotto or an herbed butter. It lends buttery flavor but is safe for those with dairy and soy sensitivities.

Dark Chocolate—In my first two books, this was a difficult ingredient, because so many chocolate companies have cross-contamination issues. Since the publication of my second book, Enjoy Life Foods has introduced Boom Choco Boom Bars in addition to their mini semisweet chocolate chips and Mega Chunks. This brand is made in a dedicated gluten-, dairy-, soy-, nut-, and egg-free facility. Sometimes, if I'm feeling particularly decadent, I like to coarsely chop this and add it to Blondies (p. 136) or Plain Old Brownies (p. 168). See the Where to Shop section (p. 182) for recommendations about where to find it.

Dijon Mustard—Be careful which mustard you use. Many types of mustard now add additional ingredients beyond the traditional ground mustard seed, vinegar, and water. Some mustards contain soy. I recommend Maille or Bournier brands for their robust flavor and lack of additives.

Flaxseed Meal—Flaxseed meal is just ground flaxseeds. I prefer the golden variety, but you can use the darker kind, too—they are the same; the golden variety is simply less visible in the finished product. One of the great things about flaxseed meal, aside from making a wonderful egg substitute in baking, is that it is also loaded with omega-3 essential fatty acids and fiber, both of which are fantastic for heart health.

French Lentils—Smaller than red and brown lentils, French lentils are green and don't get mushy during cooking. Le Puy lentils are a little more expensive, but I think that they are definitely worth the price because I strongly dislike mushy lentils.

Gluten-, Dairy-, Soy-, Nut-, and Egg-Free Chocolate Chips—When I first started baking my way around multiple food allergies, chocolate chips were a hang up. Most chocolate in this country is emulsified, or held together with soy lecithin. However, Enjoy Life Foods makes delicious dairy- and soy-free chocolate chips, chocolate chunks, and chocolate bars. They are all made in a dedicated gluten-, dairy-, soy-, nut-, and egg-free facility, which makes me feel even better about using them.

Gluten-Free All-Purpose Baking Flour—Bob's Red Mill Gluten-Free All-Purpose Baking Flour is great for baking cookies. When I want to make a cookie that spreads, like most drop cookies do, I look to this flour. It provides just the right texture and makes for a lovely, rich flavor in the finished product. Fortunately, it is easy to find at most supermarkets. However, if you cannot find it in your area, check out the company's website (www.BobsRedMill.com) to have it shipped directly to you. If you feel uncomfortable with Bob's products because of possible cross-contamination issues, Authentic Foods also makes a nice gluten-free all-purpose flour called GF (as in gluten-free) Classical Blend.

Gluten-Free Rice Milk—Some rice milks are not gluten-free because they contain barley. Make sure to check the label. If you are intolerant to coconut milk and opt to use rice milk and cider vinegar to replace cultured coconut milk in my recipes, just be sure that the rice milk you are using is 100 percent gluten-free.

Herbes de Provence—This is an herb blend that is, not surprisingly, often found in Provençal cooking. Basil, thyme, rosemary, sometimes lavender, and savory are usually included in the commercial blends.

Kasha—Do not be fooled: This is not Kashi cereal. Kasha is buckwheat groats. It is gluten-free, and while I use it in savory Kasha and Pasta (p. 102), it is also delicious served with berries and a little honey for breakfast.

Lyle's Golden Syrup—Lyle's Golden Syrup is a British baking classic that is traditionally used in treacle pudding. However, it makes a great stand-in for corn syrup if you cannot tolerate corn or just choose to avoid corn syrup in cooking. Melani Bauman, who photographed this book and is British, brought it to my attention, and I have come to rely on it for icings and sweetening some desserts.

Organic Palm Fruit Oil Shortening—In our family, shortening was always used in place of butter in our homemade chocolate chip cookies. When I started baking dairy-free, shortening was a natural fit. However, to take my recipes one step further to soy-free, I had to find a new substitute. At first this product was only available online, but now I find the Spectrum organic palm fruit oil shortening at most supermarkets. It is usually labeled "all-vegetable shortening" on the front of the tub.

Potato Starch—Potato starch is a natural thickener made from potatoes. It is especially fine and white. I use it in my baked goods to help with browning and to create a more delicate crumb in the finished product. It is not the same as potato flour, which is much heavier and will change the density of your recipes. Make sure to read the label carefully: Potato starch is bright white; potato flour is not.

Powdered Vanilla Rice Milk—Powdered vanilla rice milk revolutionized my Even Easier "Buttercream" Frosting recipe (p. 162). This ingredient added flavor, depth, and creaminess to my frosting when I felt like it was missing something. Now, frosting is so easy to make. Powdered vanilla rice milk is gluten-, dairy-, soy-, nut-, and egg-free as well as shelf stable, which makes it more economical than buying regular vanilla rice milk that I might only use in one recipe. Add a little bit of it to water mixed with apple cider vinegar as another buttermilk alternative.

Raw Coconut Aminos—This is the best ingredient I've stumbled upon in a long time. Raw coconut aminos are a great stand-in for soy sauce. They are made from coconut tree sap, which contains 17 naturally occurring amino acids—thus the name *aminos.* They are low glycemic and work well as a soy sauce stand-in in my Asian-influenced recipes.

Rose Water—Rose water is a natural flavoring that is made from rose petals and water. It is commonly used in Greek, Indian, and Middle Eastern cooking and is available, bottled, at most health food stores. Not only is it used for cooking, but some people mist rose water on their faces as a toner or spray it on their clothes when ironing to infuse its wonderful scent into the fabric. It is possible to make rose water from scratch, though, admittedly, I have never tried it, because it's so easy to find at the supermarket.

Soba Noodles—Soba noodles are Japanese noodles made from buckwheat, which is naturally gluten-free. They have a distinctive flavor that is perfect for cold noodle salads. Not all brands are gluten-free because some manufacturers blend regular wheat flour in with the buckwheat flour, so be very careful and read the label closely before purchasing.

Sorghum Flour—I love sorghum flour because when used alone it reminds me of graham flour. Denser than rice flour, sorghum flour is also gluten-free and helps keep cookies from being too crisp but keeps cakes light and moist. Sorghum is naturally a little sweeter than other flours and has a neutral flavor.

Xanthan Gum—Occasionally, I see gluten-free recipes that do not contain xanthan, and they work, but they work because they contain eggs. In allergy-free baking, xanthan is the A–No. 1, most important ingredient. Without xanthan gum, gluten- and egg-free baked goods will not rise, no matter how much leavening is added to the recipe. Xanthan replaces gluten by creating the air bubbles that pop to leave behind the delicate crumb in cakes and the chewy texture of cookies. Without this ingredient, baked goods will just look like melted blobs when they come out of the oven. Sometimes, xanthan gum is used as a thickener, though I prefer not to use it that way. Xanthan does not thicken cold liquids and can make things slippery rather than thick if not used in the right proportions.

Substitutions

The best part of writing my books is that I get to hear from so many of you! I love receiving messages from people who are equally passionate about cooking, baking, and food allergies. These conversations have taught me some important lessons over the years, such as there is no perfect food. What works for my food allergies could be deadly for another person. Also, because I live in New York City, so many ingredients are available here that may not be available everywhere. So I felt it was important to include the following list of substitutions. Thanks to your questions and comments, this list has expanded dramatically since my first and second books. Please do note, however, that the recipes in this book have only been tested as they are written and have not been tested with any of these substitute suggestions.

Before I outline substitutions for each ingredient in the book, I wanted to answer a question that belongs in this category, but doesn't fit with one specific ingredient:

What if I am not allergic to gluten but still want to make these recipes?

No problem! Just omit the xanthan gum in the recipes and use all-purpose wheat flour in place of my flour blend. For example, if the rice flour, potato starch, and sorghum flours in the recipe add up to $2\frac{1}{4}$ cups, substitute the same amount of all-purpose flour and leave out the xanthan gum.

Bob's Red Mill Gluten-Free All-Purpose Baking Flour—Per cup of all-purpose gluten-free baking flour, you may substitute $3/4$ cup superfine white rice flour plus 1 tablespoon rice flour plus $1/4$ cup plus 1 tablespoon potato starch plus 1 tablespoon plus 1 teaspoon sorghum flour. You may also substitute King Arthur Gluten-Free Multi-Purpose Flour cup for cup or the same amount of Authentic Foods GF Classical Blend. Cookies made with these substitutions may not spread as well as the cookies made with Bob's blend.

Brown Rice Couscous—Brown rice couscous is a relatively new thing that I recently stumbled across. Use it as a regular couscous or quinoa substitute.

Chile de Árbol—If you cannot find this chile pepper, just substitute red chile pepper flakes from the supermarket for a similar effect. Substitute $1/4$–$1/2$ teaspoon chile flakes per pepper, depending on your heat tolerance.

Chinese or Superfine White Rice Flour—Per 1 cup of superfine rice flour, try substituting $3/4$ cup plus 2 tablespoons sorghum or millet flour, or $3/4$ cup Bob's Red Mill All-Purpose Gluten-Free Baking Flour, or $3/4$ cup plus 2 tablespoons quinoa flour (which has a much stronger flavor than rice flour). Do *not* substitute regular-grind rice flour. It is too gritty and will alter the texture of your baked goods.

Cider Vinegar—Lemon juice or white vinegar (check that it is gluten-free) may be substituted in a direct 1:1 ratio for cider vinegar.

Coconut Milk—In most recipes, rice or soy milk can be substituted for coconut milk, though the consistency, like in a curry, will be thinner and the flavor may be lacking. In a pudding, for example, the finished product may not set up quite as well as it would with coconut milk. There is no substitute for canned coconut milk in my Whipped Cream recipe (p. 181).

Cultured Coconut Milk—If you cannot tolerate coconut or cannot find cultured coconut milk, simply use the same amount of nondairy milk of your choice or water called for in the recipe plus 1 tablespoon cider vinegar or lemon juice. If you are using water, you can also stir in 1 tablespoon powdered vanilla rice milk for flavor, but it is not required. If you are not allergic to dairy you could use buttermilk in place of the cultured coconut milk, too.

Cornstarch—Per 1 tablespoon cornstarch, you can substitute 1 tablespoon rice flour, potato flour, or potato starch; 2 teaspoons arrowroot; or 1 tablespoon tapioca starch.

Flaxseed Meal—I use flaxseed meal and water in place of eggs in some of my recipes. One egg is equal to one of the following combinations:

- 1 tablespoon flaxseed meal + 3 tablespoons water
- 1 tablespoon ground chia seeds + 3 tablespoons water
- ¼ cup unsweetened applesauce

Flour Mix—I have heard from some of you that the rice or the potato starch in my flour mix is tricky for your dietary restrictions. Substitution of a premixed flour is fine as long as it does not contain any xanthan gum, baking soda, or baking powder; these ingredients will affect the outcome of your recipe. I recommend Bob's Red Mill Gluten-Free All-Purpose Baking Flour or Authentic Foods GF Classical Blend. The texture may vary slightly from my original recipe. You may also use my Betsy's Baking Mix from my first book, *Allergy-Free Desserts.*

Gluten-Free Oats—My Kitchen Sink Cookies (p. 163) are delicious with gluten-free oats, but if your system cannot even tolerate the certified gluten-free varieties, try substituting the same amount of quinoa flakes.

Herbes de Provence—If you cannot find this in your local market, substitute fines herbes, which is a more common commercial blend. Either blend will work in my recipes that call for herbes de Provence.

Jell-O—This classic is delicious, but if you are vegan or kosher, try substituting kosher gelatin in my Cranberry Chutney Jell-O Mold recipe (p. 79). If you are vegan, opt for agar-agar, which is a made from seaweed and is 100 percent vegan.

Lyle's Golden Syrup—Light corn syrup can be substituted in a 1:1 ratio for Lyle's.

Organic Palm Fruit Oil Shortening—This is probably the most common question that I answer, and it is often because the labeling is misleading. Many organic palm fruit oil manufacturers use an "all-vegetable shortening" label, so it is unclear. The ingredients list then shows organic palm fruit oil. Often, I buy mine on Amazon if the store is out. See Where to Shop (p. 182) for places to find it. However, if you are not soy intolerant and you cannot find organic palm fruit oil shortening, Crisco is a fine substitute. I do not recommend using solid coconut oil because it tends to make recipes oily, and definitely do not use liquid oils in recipes that call for shortening because they will not turn out properly. Outside the United States, vegetable oil shortening may be known as Copha (in Australia), and Trex or White Flora (in the United Kingdom), but these may contain soy. Vegetable suet may also be substituted for organic palm fruit oil shortening; just be sure to check the label to make certain that it doesn't contain wheat.

Potato Starch—Try substituting arrowroot or tapioca starch in a direct 1:1 ratio. Do not substitute potato flour—it absolutely will not work. The outcome will be gummy and heavy.

Quinoa—If you cannot tolerate quinoa or just don't like it, try substituting Lundberg Roasted Brown Rice Couscous or cooked millet.

Soba Noodles—There are times when my usual stores are out of 100 percent buckwheat soba noodles, and then again, not everyone likes the flavor of roasted buckwheat. Try substituting Chinese glass or clear rice pasta. Bean threads would work here, too.

Sorghum—Though sorghum is easy to find in the United States, it is not as popular in other countries. Try substituting millet flour in a 1:1 ratio.

Sugar—Real sugar is necessary for creating the structure of baked goods. However, not everyone can tolerate it. These substitutions will change the texture of your finished product but they are acceptable stand-ins. Xylitol can be substituted in a direct 1:1 ratio for sugar, though it will not produce fluffy frostings. Agave may also be substituted, but in order to substitute, lower the baking temperature of the oven by 25 degrees (for example, if the recipe calls for the oven to be at 350°F, then lower it to 325°F); reduce the amount of sweetener by 25 percent (for example, if the recipe calls for 1 cup of sugar, use ³/₄ cup agave); and reduce the amount of liquid in the recipe by 25 percent (for example, if the recipe calls for 1 cup cultured coconut milk, use ³/₄ cup instead).

Sunflower Seed Butter—Sunflower seed butter is a wonderful thing for those with peanut allergies, but it does not necessarily work for everyone. If you are not soy allergic, you can substitute an equal amount of soy butter. Also, if you are peanut allergic but can tolerate tree nuts, you could use almond or cashew butter. In the event that none of these works for you but you can tolerate sesame, you could even try substituting an equal part of tahini.

Measurement Conversions for Cooks outside the United States

Outside the United States, our units of measurement don't make a whole lot of sense since they are not by weight. If you use the metric system, I've done the conversions for you. Below are my most commonly used ingredients converted to metric measurements with a few extra gluten-free flours thrown in just in case you prefer to substitute with them.

- 1 cup white rice flour = 98 grams
- 1 cup Bob's Red Mill Gluten-Free All-Purpose Flour = 151 grams
- 1 cup garbanzo flour = 115 grams
- 1 cup potato starch = 174 grams
- 1 cup granulated sugar = 198 grams
- 1 cup shortening = 190 grams
- 1 cup packed dark brown sugar = 240 grams
- 1 cup packed light brown sugar = 215 grams

Not all gluten-free flours work for everyone, and it is always nice to have options. I thought it might be helpful to list my favorite flours along with their weights so that you may use them interchangeably.

- 1 cup superfine white rice flour = 3.5 ounces
- 1 cup sorghum flour = 3.9 ounces
- 1 cup millet flour = 3.9 ounces
- 1 cup Bob's Red Mill Gluten-Free All-Purpose Flour = 5.4 ounces
- 1 cup potato starch = 6.2 ounces
- 1 cup potato flour = 6.2 ounces
- 1 cup quinoa flour = 3.4 ounces
- 1 cup garbanzo bean flour = 4.1 ounces
- 1 cup tapioca starch = 3.7 ounces
- 1 cup buckwheat flour = 4.4 ounces

main courses

Do you ever get home at night and find yourself standing in front of the fridge, scratching your head about what to serve for dinner or lunch or breakfast? I do. Usually when this happens, the children are in the background having a tantrum because they are so hungry right now. You know. You've been there. We all have. Sometimes it isn't my kids but my stomach having the tantrum, and I panic because I'm just not sure what to make. Well, thanks to my scavenging through the refrigerator and scouring the pantry, you can stop scratching your head. I've got it covered, I swear. Every dish in this section is super easy and quick to make. Many of them contain things like canned chickpeas, frozen peas, or gluten-free pasta and a few herbs—things that most of us have on hand. Other dishes are made ahead in the slow cooker, so when the kids or your stomach break down, all you'll need to do is uncover the pot and serve. Whatever the situation, I promise you good food quickly that is quality both in taste and nutrition. None of these recipes will disappoint, and I'm sure you'll find a few that will become favorites.

Bang Bang Chicken

The jury is out on why bang bang chicken is called "bang bang." Some people claim that this Szechuan street food got its name because the chicken was pounded to make it tenderer and cook faster, but I don't believe that's where it got its name. I doubt that "to hit" is *bang* in Chinese, but what do I know? My husband, Jesse, swears that the bang bang name derives from the fact that it's so quick to make that it gets "banged" out and so delicious that one "bangs" it back. I don't know the answer, and it doesn't really matter. What I do know about my Bang Bang Chicken is that it is a really great way to use leftover rotisserie chicken; it's perfect on a hot night or one on which you don't feel like cooking, and it's great to send for lunch, too. I like to offer the thinly sliced cucumber, chopped cilantro, shredded carrot, and lettuce leaves in little bowls and let everyone make their own dishes. This is something that we all look forward to and that Jesse especially asks for time and time again. Our friend Max gave me the idea, and I just tweaked his recipe ever so slightly. Since I generally have some of the Asian Dressing and Dipping Sauce in the fridge as well as a roasted chicken, I am almost always happy to oblige Jesse's frequent requests for this dish. **Serves 4**

1 pound shredded roast
   chicken
1 recipe Asian Dressing and
   Dipping Sauce (p. 116)
1 head Boston or Bibb lettuce,
   washed, dried, and whole
   leaves separated
Shredded carrot, thinly sliced
   cucumber, and chopped
   cilantro for garnish

1. Place the shredded chicken in a large bowl and add the dressing/dipping sauce. Toss the chicken to coat it completely with the sauce.

2. Place a small bit of chicken in the center of one lettuce leaf, and top with some carrot, cucumber, and a sprinkle of cilantro. Fold the lettuce around the filling and eat with your hands.

Note: If you cannot tolerate the tahini in my Asian Dressing and Dipping Sauce, substitute SunButter or homemade sunflower seed butter to make this more like a peanut sauce.

Beef Tenderloin

Every year at Christmas, my mother serves standing rib roast. I know that this is supposed to be a supreme treat and that I should love every bite. Sorry, Mom, I hate standing rib roast. But last year, we were a small group and my mother absolutely made my Christmas by deciding that it wasn't worth making standing rib roast for four adults and two finicky kids, and we instead had a tenderloin. I swear that the "Hallelujah" chorus played in the background as if on cue. This is not an everyday sort of roast, because it is essentially a giant filet mignon, and the price is generally reflective of the higher quality of the cut. However, tenderloin is easy to make, which is especially nice at the holidays when I'd rather be with my guests than in the kitchen. To me, tenderloin is worth the price a couple of times a year because the result is, in the words of Linda Richman from *Saturday Night Live,* "Like butta"—dairy-free butter that is. Ask your butcher to tie the tenderloin for you. This ensures even cooking, and it's easier if the butcher does the work. I especially like this served with my Potato and Celery Root Smash (p. 198) and a dollop of Chunky Cranberry Sauce (p. 71). SERVES **4–6**

1 tablespoon olive oil

1 teaspoon salt

Pinch of pepper

1 (2-pound) beef tenderloin roast, tied

1. Preheat the oven to 350°F. Mix together the oil, salt, and pepper, and rub the roast with the mixture.

2. Place the roast in the preheated oven with the fat side up and bake for 45 minutes. Remove the pan from the oven and let the tenderloin rest for 15 minutes before slicing.

3. Serve immediately. Leftovers may be refrigerated in an airtight container for up to three days.

Breakfast Sausage Patties

Just the other day, I was at the butcher's station at Whole Foods when someone asked about the ingredients in a particular variety of sausage. I was really surprised to hear the butcher answer that that one contained bread crumbs. I know that many varieties do contain gluten and soy, and some also contain yucky MSG, but I didn't expect to see any bread in fresh sausage. When I came home, I had sausage on the brain; after all, I'm from Ohio, home of Bob Evans! I immediately got to work. The salty spiciness of my sausage offsets the super sweetness of the syrup and waffles if you serve it with my Waffles (p. 54). I also like to crumble this, brown it, and add it to tomato sauce. Cook these sausages ahead and freeze them, then microwave for a minute before a weekday breakfast.
MAKES 8 SAUSAGE PATTIES

1. Place all ingredients in a large mixing bowl and combine them with your hands until the spices are evenly incorporated. Divide the mixture into eighths and shape into patties.

2. Heat a large skillet over medium-high heat. Add the sausage patties and cook 6–8 minutes per side until they are no longer pink in the center, and an instant-read thermometer inserted in the center reads 145°F. Serve immediately.

3. The leftovers may be refrigerated in an airtight container for up to three days, or the completely cooled leftovers may be frozen in airtight containers for up to three months.

2 pounds ground pork
2 teaspoons Italian seasoning
1 teaspoon salt
1/2 teaspoon fennel seeds
1/2 teaspoon red chile flakes
1/4 teaspoon black pepper

Beef Tostadas

I originally intended this recipe to be something a bit fancier, something made with flank steak cooked on the grill and then wrapped in soft corn tortillas. My girls had different plans for a taco recipe and turned up their noses at the idea of anything short of hard taco shells and ground beef. Since I didn't feel like eating a traditional taco, I went with the tostada shells that I had in the cupboard. This spicy stovetop recipe is really quick to cook. Bring bowls of shredded lettuce, Guacamole (p. 88), Black Bean Salsa (p. 68), and Daiya cheese to the table, and let everyone put them together themselves. They make for a fun Tex-Mex fiesta. **Serves 4**

¼ teaspoon chipotle chile powder
½ teaspoon garlic salt
¼ teaspoon onion salt
1 teaspoon dried oregano
1 teaspoons ground cumin
¼ teaspoon salt
1 pound ground sirloin
8 gluten- and soy-free corn tostadas
Diced tomato, avocado, red onion, Daiya cheese, shredded lettuce, and cilantro for serving (optional)

1. In a small bowl, stir together the chipotle chile powder, garlic salt, onion salt, dried oregano, cumin, and salt. Set aside.

2. In a large skillet, brown the beef over medium-high heat until it is cooked through, about 10 minutes, stirring frequently to break up any large chunks of meat.

3. Remove the beef from the heat and drain off the fat. Sprinkle with the spice mix and stir so that the spices are evenly incorporated. Spoon the meat into the tostada shells and serve immediately, garnished as desired.

4. The unused meat may be refrigerated in an airtight container for up to three days.

Note: I had a hard time finding soybean oil–free tostada shells in my market. To make your own, take corn tortillas and fry them in 3–4 inches of canola oil heated to 350°F for about 2 minutes or until they are crisp and golden. Remove the fried tortillas to a paper towel-lined tray to drain.

Note: When working with hot oil, be sure to use a candy thermometer to ensure an accurate cooking temperature.

Brisket

Though brisket is great on Rosh Hashanah, I could eat it every day of the year. This is a super-simple, hands-off recipe that I make at least once a week. I put it in the slow cooker before I go out for the day and come home to a perfect dinner. Add a green salad and a baked potato and you have almost no cleanup and a balanced dinner with only about ten minutes of prep work. All you need is a slow cooker to facilitate the meal. This moist and tender brisket makes great leftovers!
SERVES 4

1 (1½-pound) beef brisket (not corned beef)
1 cup gluten-free beef stock
2 medium onions (about 1 pound), cut into wedges
1 large, peeled carrot, sliced
1 stalk celery, sliced
1 teaspoon salt

1. Place the brisket in the bottom of a 3-quart slow cooker. It will be a tight squeeze, but it will fit. Add the stock, onions, carrots, celery, and salt and turn the slow cooker to low.

2. Cook the brisket on low for 9 hours or until the brisket is fork-tender. Remove from the slow cooker, slice it very thinly against the grain, and serve with the onions, carrots, and celery.

3. Leftovers may be refrigerated in an airtight container for up to three days.

Indian Rice Pudding

I know that pudding seems like a strange main course, but honestly, it's a nice departure from your average gluten-free oatmeal, and I love to have a hot meal first thing in the morning. You might notice that I intentionally left sugar out of this recipe, because I like the idea of a DIY! When I was a girl, my mother always had a sugar bowl on the breakfast table so that we could sweeten our cereal or cinnamon toast as desired. My brother was very sensible and only sprinkled a spoonful over his Rice Chex. I wasn't as sensible, and more often than not I added the entire sugar bowl. When I lived in Germany, we ate *Milchreis* for dinner, which is essentially rice pudding made with arborio rice, and whenever a German made it for me, it was served with sugar on the side. I loved sprinkling sugar on top because, added at the end, the sugar gave my rice a delicate crunch, and I liked being able to control the sweetness. Obviously, I had developed a hint of self-restraint by then. This Indian rice pudding has the traditional flavors of delicate rose water and powerful cardamom. If you can't find rose water or just don't think it sounds tasty, feel free to substitute a teaspoon of vanilla extract and one cinnamon stick for the cardamom pods. Add a drizzle of honey or sprinkle of sugar before enjoying. Serves **4–6**

1. Combine the coconut milk, water, rice, salt, and cardamom pods in a large, heavy-bottomed pot. Set the pot over medium-high heat and bring the liquid just to a boil (large bubbles will just begin to form and burst, but it should not be a full, rolling boil). Reduce the heat to low and cook the pudding, uncovered, for about 2 hours, or until the pudding is thick and the rice is tender, stirring occasionally.

2. Carefully remove and discard the cardamom pods and transfer the pudding to a serving bowl. Serve the pudding immediately, or, if you prefer cold rice pudding like I do, press a piece of plastic wrap directly on top of the pudding and refrigerate until it is chilled. Drizzle with honey or sprinkle with sugar before serving. Leftovers may be refrigerated in an airtight container for up to five days.

$3^1/_2$ cups well-shaken, room-temperature coconut milk (about 3 14-ounce cans)
2 cups water
$3/_4$ cup basmati rice
$1/_4$ teaspoon salt
3 whole cardamom pods
$3/_4$ teaspoon rose water
Sugar or honey for serving

Note: This also tastes great with my Stewed Fruit (p. 48) on top.

Chicken Brochettes Provençal

When I lived in France, the arrival of the Beaujolais Nouveau was practically a national holiday. Really, when this table wine came out every year, there was always a celebration. Though I doubt that anyone served these brochettes, they are inspired by my time abroad. I love the cozy combination of the tomatoes and olives, and the fresh parsley adds just the right amount of refreshing zing. All three are flavors associated with the south of France, and when served up with either Beaujolais Nouveau in the late fall or Rosé in the summer, they make a deliciously light and simple meal. They pair beautifully with Soft Polenta (p. 108) and a simple salad dressed with Sherry Vinaigrette (p. 124). SERVES 4 GENEROUSLY

1 (10-ounce) jar sun-dried tomatoes packed in oil
2 cloves garlic, minced
$\frac{1}{2}$ cup pitted black olives, finely diced
$\frac{1}{4}$ cup loosely packed, roughly chopped Italian parsley leaves
$\frac{3}{4}$ teaspoon salt
2 pounds cubed boneless, skinless chicken breast
8 wooden skewers

1. Soak eight wooden skewers in water for 30 minutes.

2. Place the sun-dried tomatoes, their oil, and the garlic in the bowl of a food processor and pulse until they form a thick paste. Add the black olives and Italian parsley and pulse five or six times, until they are roughly chopped.

3. Add the chicken to a large bowl and pour the tomato mixture over the top. Using your hands, make sure that all sides of the chicken are coated with the tomato mixture. Thread the chicken cubes onto the soaked skewers and place them on a tray or baking sheet. Top with any remaining sauce, cover with plastic wrap, and let marinate for 1 hour.

4. Preheat a gas grill to high or a lightly oiled grill pan over high heat. Place the brochettes on the grill or grill pan and reduce the heat to medium. Cover and cook for 12 minutes. Turn the brochettes and cook, covered, another 8 minutes.

5. Serve immediately. Leftovers may be refrigerated in an airtight container for up to three days.

Note: The brochettes may be broiled if you prefer.

Note: If you use your hands to mix the raw chicken and the marinade, be sure to wash your hands very thoroughly when you are finished to avoid salmonella contamination.

Chicken Charmoula with Roasted Potatoes

Our friend Eve makes the most incredible chicken charmoula I've ever tasted. In fact, I had never had charmoula until she made it at our friend Lucy's house. However, one bite and I was hooked. The sauce is light and herby with a kick, and the secret is the piment d'Espelette. This is a spice that can be difficult to track down, but if you can't find it in your neighborhood, you can get it from Kalustyan's in New York City; call them at (800) 352-3451. Marinating the chicken in this sauce makes it so juicy and delicious! Not in the mood for potatoes? This chicken also pairs perfectly with my One-Pot Quinoa with Spinach, Pomegranate, and Yam (p. 32). Try making the potatoes without the chicken as a delicious side at Thanksgiving. **SERVES 4**

2 cloves garlic, minced
½ cup chopped fresh Italian parsley
½ cup chopped fresh cilantro leaves
1 teaspoon ground cumin
1 teaspoon piment d'Espelette
1 teaspoon red wine vinegar
¾ cup olive oil
1 teaspoon kosher salt
1 (3-pound) chicken, quartered
2 pounds scrubbed and quartered new potatoes

1. In a small bowl, make the charmoula by whisking together the garlic, parsley, cilantro, cumin, piment d'Espelette, red wine vinegar, olive oil, and salt.

2. Place the chicken in a roasting pan and cover it with the charmoula. Cover the baking dish with plastic wrap and let it marinate in the refrigerator for at least 4 hours or overnight.

3. Preheat the oven to 400°F.

4. Remove the chicken from the refrigerator and remove the plastic wrap. Add the potatoes to the roasting pan and toss to coat with the charmoula sauce that has pooled in the bottom of the roasting pan. Place the roasting pan in the preheated oven.

5. Bake for 50 minutes or until juices run clear when cutting into the thickest part of the chicken breast and the internal temperature reads 165°F with an instant-read thermometer.

6. Serve immediately. Refrigerate leftovers in an airtight container for up to three days.

Chicken Posole

I love this soup because it contains three of my favorite things: hominy, lime, and cilantro. And I love it because it pairs particularly well with corn chips. Yum! What makes this really great, though, is that it takes under 15 minutes to cook and it makes 8 to 10 servings, so I can freeze half for later. I love to make a whole chicken at the beginning of the week and have my family work our way through it all week long, but there are many times when I'm pressed for time and need to get something to the table quickly. (I assume that you find yourself in this situation from time to time as well.) So, when this happens, I rely on a good, old-fashioned rotisserie chicken to save the day. And that's exactly what I recommend for this recipe. I only use one dried pepper in this recipe because my children don't like spicy food. Take it up a notch with additional pepper if your crew likes to get spicy. Olé! SERVES 8–10

2 tablespoons olive oil

$^3/_4$ cup diced yellow onion (about 1 small/medium onion)

3 cloves garlic, minced

2 teaspoons salt

2 tablespoons dried oregano

1 dried red chile pepper (chile de árbol), chopped

1 (28-ounce) can crushed tomatoes in thick puree

8 cups chicken stock

1 (3-pound) cooked rotisserie chicken, deboned and meat shredded (about 1 pound meat)

2 (15-ounce) cans hominy, drained

$^1/_4$ cup lime juice

$^1/_2$ cup chopped cilantro leaves

1. In a large stock pot, heat the olive oil over medium-high heat. Add the onions and garlic and sauté until they are soft and translucent, about 5 minutes.

2. Add the salt, oregano, red chile pepper, crushed tomatoes, chicken stock, chicken, and hominy. Stir to combine the ingredients and bring to a simmer. Simmer for 3–5 minutes or until the soup is hot and the chicken and hominy are warmed through. Remove from the heat and stir in the lime juice and cilantro.

3. Serve immediately. Leftovers may be refrigerated in an airtight container for up to five days, or the fully cooled soup may be frozen in airtight containers for up to three months.

Cobb Salad

I'm not exactly sure why, but when my first daughter, Margot, was born, I craved cobb salads endlessly. It was like a modern-day scene from Rapunzel. I would have scaled a wall and dealt with a witch just to get my hands on the cobb salad from Fred's, a restaurant on the Upper West Side of Manhattan. Ever since those first few days home from the hospital, I have added cobb salad to my summer repertoire. Oddly, before the cravings, this was not a salad that I had ever really fancied, but now I find it the perfect light, summertime lunch and a nice addition to a Fourth of July picnic, since that is when the corn on Long Island is at its peak. **SERVES 6**

5 slices bacon

4 cups mixed greens, washed

½ cup diced orange or red bell pepper (about ½ medium)

½ cup sliced cherry tomatoes (cut into thirds)

¼ cup grated carrots

¼ cup diced red onion

1 cup fresh corn kernels (from about 2 ears of corn), cooked

10 pitted black olives

8 ounces cooked, diced chicken breast

½ ripe avocado, peeled and diced

1 recipe Simple Vinaigrette (p. 125)

1. Place the bacon in a heavy skillet. (I prefer cast iron.) Cook over medium-high heat, turning frequently, to desired crispness. Remove to a paper towel–lined plate to cool. When the bacon is cool enough to handle, crumble it.

2. Meanwhile, place the mixed greens, bell pepper, cherry tomatoes, grated carrots, red onion, corn kernels, olives, chicken, and avocado in a large salad bowl.

3. Add the bacon and the vinaigrette and toss to evenly distribute the chopped vegetables, meat, and dressing. Serve immediately.

Creamy Thai Coconut Chicken

This might be my favorite savory dish in this whole book. I just love the way that the creaminess of the rice and the punch of the Green Curry Paste (p. 120) complement each other. I add thinly sliced carrots for color, but you could also use red bell pepper or even a cup of a frozen pepper-and-onion mix if you're really short on time. If you can tolerate shellfish, you could make this with shrimp instead of chicken. So many options! What I really love about this dinner is that it is a one-pot wonder, and in most cases it makes enough for dinner tonight and lunch tomorrow. Throw everything in, stir it up, and put it in the oven. Voilà! Dinner is on the table in about 35 minutes, including prep time. **SERVES 6**

1 tablespoon olive oil
$\frac{1}{2}$ cup diced onion
1 cup thinly sliced carrot or
   diced red pepper
2 pounds chicken breast cut
   into $\frac{1}{2}$-inch chunks
2 cups basmati rice
1 (13.5-ounce) can coconut milk
   (not light)
2$\frac{1}{2}$ cups water
1 cup Green Curry Paste (p.
   120)
Salt to taste

1. Preheat the oven to 350°F. Add the olive oil to a dutch oven or a large pot fitted with a lid, and heat over medium-high heat. Add the diced onion and the carrots or peppers and cook until the onions are soft and translucent, but not browned at the edges, about 5–7 minutes.

2. Add the chicken and stir, cooking for about 2 minutes. The edges should just be turning opaque. Add the rice, coconut milk, and water, and turn the heat up to high. Bring the mixture to a full boil, cover the pot with the lid, and place it in the preheated oven.

3. Bake the rice and vegetables for 25 minutes. Remove the pot from the oven and stir in the Green Curry Paste. Taste and season to taste with salt if necessary. Serve immediately.

4. Leftovers may be refrigerated in an airtight container for three to five days.

Dilled Rice with Lima Beans

My friend Neda is Persian, and when we were kids, I loved to go to her house for dinner because her mother cooked things that were so different than what my family ate every night. When we were in the ninth grade, Neda invited four of our friends, myself included, over for dinner, and her mother made a dish that has literally stuck with me since that night. I only ate it that one time, but I thought about it frequently until this past summer. I realized that I could probably convince her mother to teach me how to make it. So, when I went home for a visit, I called Neda's mom and described this dilled rice dish that she had served us so long ago. She was not only tickled that I had remembered this vegetarian main course but also was thrilled to teach me how to make it. I had such a great time with her that morning. I took lots of photos and learned how to make the best part of any Persian rice dish—the crispy crust, which is known as *tah dig* in Farsi. Your family will be fighting over every last crunchy bite. Once you make rice this way, you'll never want to use the American method again. Don't be intimidated by a new technique. After you do this once, it will feel like old hat. I prefer to use a pot with a tightly fitted glass top for this recipe so that I can check for the steam and make sure the rice is not burning. **Serves 6**

10 cups water

2 cups long-grain American white rice, like Texmati

1 tablespoon salt

1½ cups fresh dill, coarsely chopped

1 teaspoon ground turmeric

2 tablespoons olive oil

¼ cup grapeseed or canola oil

¼ cup dairy- and soy-free margarine (see Where to Shop, p. 182)

¼ cup dried dill

½ teaspoon salt

1 (10-ounce) package frozen lima beans, unthawed

1. Combine the water, rice, salt, fresh dill, turmeric, and olive oil in a very large pot with a tightly fitting glass lid. Bring to a boil, and boil, uncovered, for 7 minutes. The rice will be tender but not fully cooked. Remove from the heat and drain the rice in a large colander. Rinse the rice with cold water and let it cool for about 5 minutes. Do not worry about rinsing away the dill—you won't—or the turmeric, which is there mostly for color. It also will not rinse out.

2. Return the empty pot to the stove and add the grapeseed or canola oil. Place 3 cups cooled rice into the pan and press it down with a spatula to pack it tightly into the bottom of the pan to form a crust. Cover the pressed rice with the dried dill and then pile the rest of the drained rice and fresh dill mixture into the pan. Using the tip of a wooden spoon handle, poke about 5 holes in the pile of rice. This will allow steam to escape and cook the rice. Add the margarine to the top of the pile. There is no need to stir it in. Sprinkle with the salt.

3. Turn up the heat to medium-high and cover the pot. Watch closely that steam is coming up and that the rice is steaming, not burning. Cook on medium-high for 10 minutes. If the rice begins to burn, reduce the heat.

4. Reduce the heat to medium. Uncover the pot and, being careful not to burn yourself, place a clean dishcloth or double layer of paper towels over the top of the pot and then replace the lid. The presence of the paper towels allows the rice to steam in the pot. Fold the ends of the towels up over the pot so they do not catch on fire. Continue cooking over medium heat for 30 minutes.

5. Add the lima beans during the last 10 minutes of cooking.

6. Remove the rice from the heat and fluff with a fork to mix in the lima beans. Pile the rice into a large serving dish (I like to use a paella pan or tagine) and carefully lift the *tah dig* (the crunchy rice crust) out of the bottom of the pot with a metal spatula. Do not be alarmed if it breaks into pieces. It is sometimes difficult to remove, and pieces of it are fine. Pile it on top of the rice. Serve immediately for maximum crispiness.

7. Leftovers may be refrigerated in an airtight container for up to three days.

Green Chili

I have found that the key to a really good party is actually being there. I have hosted many a party from the kitchen because I was chained to the stove, tending to the meal. Those parties weren't fun, and by the end of the night I was tired and grumpy, not the way that I like to feel at the end of the party. I discovered that if I took a more hands-off approach, either by encouraging friends to bring something or by using my slow cooker, parties were a lot more fun. I created this chili recipe for just that reason. This feeds a lot of people even though I make it in my teeny, tiny slow cooker. Yes, this cook only has a three-quart slow cooker. Nevertheless, this stew is spicy and hearty, and it takes all of about 10 minutes to put together. Put the ingredients in the night before, refrigerate, then set your alarm for a 7:00 a.m. wake up, plug it in, and go back to bed. By dinnertime you'll have a perfectly braised green chili and won't have to think twice about it. I like that kind of main course. This is my daughter Margot's favorite recipe in the book, and she asks me to make it at least once a week in the winter. I just freeze the leftovers. Serves **10–12**

3 pounds boneless pork butt, cubed

1 tablespoon dried oregano

2 teaspoons ground cumin

1 cup diced yellow onion (about 1 medium)

2 (15-ounce) cans crushed tomatillos

1 (4-ounce) can diced mild green chiles

1 teaspoon salt

2 cups chopped fresh cilantro leaves (about 2 bunches)

Cooked white rice, diced jalapeños, and lime wedges for serving

1. Add the cubed pork, oregano, cumin, onion, tomatillos, chiles, and salt to a 3-quart slow cooker.

2. Set the slow cooker to low and cook for 12 hours or until the pork is fork-tender. Stir in the cilantro leaves.

3. Serve with rice, limes, and diced jalapeños. Leftovers may be refrigerated in an airtight container for up to three days. Alternatively, completely cooled leftovers may be frozen in airtight containers for up to three months.

Note: If you did set your alarm clock and are taking the ingredients and the slow cooker's ceramic insert out of the refrigerator, you may need to add a little additional cooking time to account for preheating, usually 30 minutes at the most.

Kielbasa Kebabs

Not long ago, my youngest daughter came home from school and told me about her favorite class: health. Sometimes these conversations get a little detailed, if you know what I mean, so I braced myself for a discussion of the birds and the bees. Fortunately, Colombe just wanted to tell me that the health teacher had discussed good nutrition with her class. She told the children that one of the best ways to fill their nutritional needs was by filling a plate with as many different colors as possible. I thought this was sound advice! These kebabs fit the bill. They are bright and colorful, and take almost no time to prepare and even less time to cook. These are a great dinner on a cold winter night because they are so bright and cheerful. They are also delicious as a summer lunch. I chose this combination of vegetables because it appealed to me, but feel free to use what you have on hand or whatever is in season. I am not fond of mushrooms, but button mushrooms, yellow squash, eggplant, or any number of vegetables would make a great addition to this mélange. With the exception of blue, I believe that every color of the rainbow is represented here. I think that Colombe's health teacher would be satisfied. To incorporate every color of the spectrum into the meal, serve boiled blue potatoes instead of rice on the side. Serves 4

$\frac{1}{2}$ pint grape tomatoes (about 6 ounces)

$\frac{1}{2}$ large red onion (about 5 ounces), peeled and cut into wedges and then into thirds

1 medium zucchini (about 10 ounces), cut into disks

3 bell peppers, mixed colors (about 10 ounces), cut into 1$\frac{1}{2}$-inch squares

1 tablespoon olive oil

1 (14-ounce) fully cooked kielbasa, sliced into $\frac{1}{2}$-inch coins

Basmati rice for serving (optional)

8 wooden skewers

1. Soak eight wooden skewers in water for 30 minutes.

2. Place the vegetables in a large bowl and toss them with the olive oil to coat.

3. Thread a tomato, an onion wedge, a zucchini disk, a piece of pepper, and a slice of kielbasa onto a soaked skewer. Repeat the pattern until the entire skewer is threaded. Place the kebab on a broiling pan. Continue with this process until all of the skewers are threaded and no vegetables or sausage remains.

4. Preheat the broiler. Place the broiler pan under the broiler and cook for 4 minutes. Turn the kebabs and cook for another 4 minutes. Serve immediately over rice. Leftovers may be tightly wrapped and refrigerated for up to three days.

Lunchtime Snow Pea Salad

I make this at lunch because it only takes about 10 minutes, but you can make it any time you feel like enjoying crunchy sweet snow peas, English peas, and crispy bacon. My local market sells fresh peas that have been shelled, but since most markets don't, I made the recipe with frozen peas. **Serves 4**

5 slices bacon
1 cup frozen peas, unthawed
1 pound fresh snow peas
¼ cup Simple Vinaigrette
    (p. 125)

1. Place the strips of bacon in a pan and cook them over medium-low heat, turning often, until crisp, about 10–15 minutes. Remove the bacon with tongs to a plate lined with paper towels to drain. Set aside.

2. Place a steamer basket in the bottom of a medium pot fitted with a lid, and fill the pot with about 2–3 inches of water; the water should not come above the steamer basket. Bring the water to a boil over high heat. Add the frozen peas and the snow peas and cover the pot. Steam the peas for 3 minutes. Remove them from the heat and rinse with cold water to stop the cooking. Gently pat the peas dry with paper towels and transfer them to a large salad bowl.

3. Pour the vinaigrette over the salad. Toss to coat and divide between four plates. Crumble the bacon and sprinkle over each salad. Serve immediately.

Meat and Veggie Meat Loaf

One day I was craving meat loaf, and I had two pounds of meat that I needed to use up. At the time, my husband was dieting and my girls were on a boycott of any vegetables other than carrots. Looking around in the fridge, I figured I'd throw in some shredded zucchini because it was the end of the week, and I needed to polish it off. I also had some mushrooms, so I figured why not? If I just pureed the vegetables, the girls would not be the wiser, and my husband would save on calories. Using a little cornstarch to bind the whole thing, it just worked, and I have forever ditched any other method of making meat loaf. This dish is savory, delicious, and loaded with the good stuff: lean protein, lots of vegetables, and plenty of flavor. If you get tired of the turkey and beef mix, try using a traditional meat loaf mix of veal, pork, and beef. My girls love this with Roasted String Beans (p. 113) and Rösti (p. 106). I love that I can make one for tonight and freeze one for later.

MAKES TWO 9 x 5-INCH LOAVES

Canola oil

1 (10-ounce) package cremini or portobello mushrooms, washed well

2 cloves garlic

1 small/medium onion (about 8 ounces)

1 small zucchini (about 6½ ounces)

1 teaspoon salt

1 tablespoon Italian seasoning

⅓ cup ketchup, plus more if desired

1 tablespoon raw coconut aminos

1 tablespoon cornstarch or potato starch

1 pound ground dark meat turkey (93 percent lean)

1 pound ground sirloin (90 percent lean)

1. Preheat the oven to 400°F and very lightly grease two 9 x 5-inch loaf pans with canola oil.

2. Add the cleaned mushrooms, garlic, onion, zucchini, salt, Italian seasoning, ⅓ cup ketchup, coconut aminos, and cornstarch or potato starch to the bowl of a food processor and process them until pureed.

3. Place the ground turkey and sirloin in a large mixing bowl and add the vegetable puree. Using your hands, work them together until the ingredients are evenly distributed.

4. Spoon the mixture into the prepared pans and spread with additional ketchup, if desired.

5. Bake in the preheated oven for 50 minutes. Remove the finished meat loaves from the oven and pour off any oil. Let them cool in the pans for 10 minutes before serving.

6. Leftovers may be refrigerated in an airtight container for three to five days. Alternatively, the fully cooled meat loaves may be frozen in an airtight container for up to three months.

Mexican Chicken Burgers

These spicy burgers make me want to say olé! I love the smoky heat of the chipotle chile pepper, and I try to serve these as often as possible for my husband and me. Serve them on gluten-, dairy-, soy-, nut-, and egg-free hamburger buns or just with a side of corn chips. These festive burgers are great for Cinco de Mayo, but I often whip up a smaller batch for dinner throughout the year because they are so quick and easy to make. If they are too spicy for your littlest diners, halve the amount of chipotle pepper. **SERVES 4**

1. Lightly grease a grill pan with canola oil and preheat over high heat.

2. Combine all of the ingredients except buns, avocado, and tomato in a large bowl and form into four patties.

3. Place the patties on the preheated grill and lower the heat to medium-high. Cook the burgers for 6 minutes per side or until they are cooked through and the internal temperature reads 165°F with an instant-read thermometer.

4. Serve immediately on the buns if you are using them. Top with avocado and tomato slices.

5. Leftovers may be refrigerated in airtight containers for up to three days.

Canola oil
1 pound ground chicken
1³/₄ teaspoons finely chopped chipotle chile pepper in adobo sauce
1 clove garlic, minced
Zest of 1 lime
1 teaspoon cumin
¹/₂ teaspoon salt
Pinch of pepper
¹/₄ cup loosely packed cilantro leaves, chopped
¹/₂ teaspoon lime juice
4 gluten-, dairy-, soy-, nut-, and egg-free hamburger buns
Avocado and tomato slices for serving

One-Pot Quinoa with Spinach, Pomegranate, and Yam

This is a terrific main course salad to serve for any meal because it is not only entirely vegetarian but also complete nutrition in one pot. This warm quinoa salad is also colorful and therefore beautiful to behold. By the way, all of the ingredients are really good for the ticker, which I'm always considering when it comes to my husband. I originally intended this to be a couscous made with brown rice couscous, which you could definitely substitute for the quinoa, but I used quinoa instead since it is the only grain that is also a complete protein. I love a one-pot meal, and believe it or not, I usually eat this one for breakfast. Though a bit more expensive, I am lazy and like to buy the pomegranate arils precut at the supermarket to save time. Often, if I know that I am making this salad, I bake the yam the night before and let it chill overnight so that it's ready to handle in the morning. SERVES 4

1 (4-ounce) yam, scrubbed
2 cups quinoa
4 cups cold water
1³/₄ teaspoons salt
3 ounces baby spinach (about 2 cups, loosely packed)
3 tablespoons pomegranate arils
2 tablespoons olive oil
2 tablespoons lemon juice
1 tablespoon chopped fresh dill

1. Preheat the oven to 400°F and bake the yam in its skin for 45 minutes or until it is tender. Remove from the oven and let the yam rest until it is cool enough to handle. Remove the skin and cut the yam into cubes.

2. Pour the quinoa into a fine-mesh sieve and rinse it with cold water until the water runs clear, about 2 minutes. After the quinoa is rinsed, pour it into a pot, cover it with 4 cups water, and add the salt. Bring the water to a boil and then reduce the heat to a simmer. Simmer the quinoa for 12 minutes and then stir in the baby spinach. Continue to simmer for another 3 minutes. Drain the quinoa and spinach in a fine-mesh sieve and transfer it to a large serving bowl. Add the cubed yam and pomegranate arils.

3. In a small separate bowl, whisk together the olive oil and lemon juice to create a vinaigrette. Pour the vinaigrette over the quinoa salad and toss to coat. Sprinkle with the dill and serve immediately.

4. Leftovers may be refrigerated in an airtight container for up to three days.

Poached Salmon

Here's a funny story about the first time I tried to serve poached salmon at a big party: It was a complete and total disaster. My first mistake was using a pan that was too small. I couldn't get the whole fish out of the small pan, and it all fell apart. It was also horribly overcooked. My guests politely nibbled on their overcooked salmon slop, while I pretended that I had intended for it to come out that way. After all, didn't Julia Child say that we should never apologize at the table? Well, I can tell you that I may not have apologized at the table, but I sure wanted to crawl under it. Of course, I meant this meal to impress. It did not. That day I learned the cardinal rule of cooking: Never serve anything at a party that you haven't made before. Now I've made this recipe so many times that I can laugh about it. In fact, I love to make this on a Friday afternoon in the summertime, let it chill overnight, and then take it down to the beach for a nice picnic with my French Lentil Salad (p. 82) and a green salad. Whether you choose to serve this hot or cold, it is always an easy feast to bring to the table, and once you get the hang of poaching salmon, it will always impress. Use any leftovers for my Salmon Croquettes (p. 42) or keep them in the fridge for a super-quick lunch. **Serves 4**

8 cups water

1½ cups dry white wine

1–2 large yellow onions (about 1 pound), quartered

2 large carrots, peeled but left whole

1 tablespoon whole peppercorns

1½ pounds boneless salmon fillet, 1½ inches thick, with skin on

1 teaspoon salt

Dill for garnish (optional)

Note: The trick to poaching salmon is to poach the fish for 10 minutes per 1 inch of thickness, so it is worth measuring the salmon's thickness before beginning.

1. Fill a large skillet fitted with a lid with the water, wine, onion, carrots, and peppercorns, place it over high heat, and bring to a boil. If your fish is too long for a skillet, you could also use a roasting pan set over two burners and sheets of aluminum foil in place of the lid.

2. While the water comes to a boil, place the fish, skin side down, on a very long sheet of aluminum foil with holes poked in it, one that allows for a 2-inch overhang on either end of the skillet. Rub the salmon fillet with the salt.

3. When the water is at a full, rolling boil, carefully lower the fish on the sheet of foil into the boiling liquid, reduce the heat, and simmer the fish for 2 minutes. Turn off the heat entirely, remove the skillet from the burner, and tightly cover it. Let the fish poach for 16 minutes.

4. Carefully take the edges of the aluminum and lift the fish out of the poaching liquid, placing the foil and fish on a platter. Remove the aluminum foil from the bottom of the fish—the skin may come off too, which is fine—and discard the foil and skin if it has come off. Return the fish to a serving platter. Discard the poaching liquid or strain it and reserve it for another use. Serve the fish immediately or move it to the refrigerator to chill completely before serving. Sprinkle with a little fresh dill just before serving.

5. Leftovers may be refrigerated in an airtight container for up to three days.

Polenta Pizza

I was about to write that I don't know anyone who doesn't like pizza, but then I realized that would be lying: My oldest daughter, Margot, is not a big pizza fan. I find that ironic because I ate a whole lot of pizza when I was pregnant with her! Margot's preferences aside, I think it's safe to say that the overwhelming majority of American families like pizza, and that most people with food allergies feel somewhat deprived if they have to give it up. I know I did. I wanted to make a recipe that was really quick and easy. Polenta was the obvious solution. The other thing that I like about polenta pizza is that the "crust" can be made ahead of time, chilled, and cut into disks with a round cookie cutter or rim of a glass. Then everyone can top their own mini pizza! Use my topping suggestions as a guideline. Every family has different preferences. These are ours. **SERVES 4–6**

1 recipe Soft Polenta (p. 108)

1 tablespoon olive oil

5 ounces frozen, chopped spinach, thawed, all the water squeezed out

10 sun-dried tomatoes in oil, drained and chopped

10 canned artichoke quarters, drained

5 black olives, pitted and halved

4 ounces chopped ham

½ teaspoon Italian seasoning

Daiya or other dairy-free cheese of your choice (optional)

1. Prepare the Soft Polenta according to the recipe directions.

2. Pour the polenta into a lightly greased 15-inch round pizza pan. The crust should be about ½ inch thick, and you may have a little polenta left over. Refrigerate the leftovers in an airtight container for up to 5 days for a later use. Place the poured polenta in the refrigerator for at least an hour, preferably overnight, to cool completely.

3. Preheat the oven to 450°F. Remove the pan from the refrigerator and brush the polenta with the olive oil. Place the pizza pan in the oven and bake the crust for 20 minutes; the edges should just begin to brown.

4. Spread the spinach, tomatoes, artichoke quarters, black olives, and ham over the crust and sprinkle the top with Italian seasoning and Daiya or other allergy-free cheese, if desired. Bake the pizza in the preheated oven for 6 more minutes. Let the pizza set for 10 minutes before cutting into wedges and serving.

5. Leftovers may be tightly wrapped and refrigerated for up to five days.

NOTE: To make these even more fun, turn them into individual pizzas. Pour the Soft Polenta into a rimmed baking sheet and place it in the refrigerator to chill and set for about 3 hours. Using a 3-inch round cookie cutter or a greased glass rim, cut out mini pizzas and carefully move the rounds to a lightly greased baking sheet. Bake according to the recipe instructions.

Pork Tenderloin with Roasted Apples, Onions, and Fennel

I like to make dinners that require as little cleanup as possible, and this is one of my go-to favorites. Just toss the vegetables and pork with a little salt and olive oil and bake them up. I usually combine the vegetables with oil in a separate bowl, but you could do everything on one baking sheet to make cleanup even faster. This autumnal dish is sweet and savory all at once. When served with a baked potato or Soft Polenta (p. 108), it always hits the spot after a long fall day. SERVES 4

1 fennel bulb (about 1 pound), fronds and core removed, cut into wedges

1 small yellow onion (about 4 ounces), cut in wedges

1 pound red apples, peeled, cored, and sliced (about 2 large apples)

1 pound trimmed pork tenderloin

1 tablespoon plus 1 teaspoon olive oil

1 teaspoon salt, divided

1. Preheat the oven to 400°F.

2. In a large bowl toss the fennel, onion, and apple slices with 1 tablespoon olive oil and ½ teaspoon salt. Dump the vegetable and apple mixture out onto a rimmed baking sheet so that the slices are arranged in a single layer. Roast in the preheated oven for 10 minutes.

3. While the fennel, onion, and apple are roasting, rub the pork tenderloin with the remaining olive oil and salt.

4. When 10 minutes are up, take the baking sheet out of the oven, push the vegetables to one side, and place the tenderloin on the other side of the baking sheet. Return the baking sheet to the oven and roast for 35 more minutes, stirring the vegetables twice during cooking to prevent burning.

5. Remove the baking sheet from the oven and let the pork tenderloin rest for 10 minutes before slicing it. Serve immediately.

6. Leftovers may be refrigerated in an airtight container for up to five days.

Risotto with Roasted Squash and Sage

Risotto is such a versatile addition to any family's menu, which is one of the reasons that I like it so much. With butternut squash and sage, this dish is perfect as a side or a vegetarian main course. The best part is that it's really a two for one: Make the risotto tonight and turn the leftovers into risotto cakes the next day by forming handfuls of risotto into patties; coating them with gluten, dairy-, soy-, nut-, and egg-free crisped rice cereal like Erewhon; and frying them in olive oil for 4 minutes per side. With time more precious than ever and the high cost of food these days, I love anything that saves time and money. This is a recipe that does both. The flavor combo pairs nicely with turkey, so I have even served this as a side at Thanksgiving! SERVES 4 GENEROUSLY

3 tablespoons olive oil, divided

1 pound peeled and diced butternut squash

5 cups chicken stock

$\frac{1}{2}$ teaspoon salt

1 clove garlic, minced

1 cup arborio rice

$\frac{1}{4}$ cup white cooking wine

2 tablespoon dairy- and soy-free margarine (see Where to Shop, p. 182)

$\frac{1}{2}$ teaspoon dried sage

1. Heat 2 tablespoons olive oil in a large skillet over medium-high heat. Add the diced squash and sauté about 12 minutes, or until tender. Transfer to a plate. Wipe out the inside of the pan.

2. Meanwhile, in a saucepan, heat the chicken stock and salt over medium heat to a simmer. Reduce the heat to low to keep warm.

3. While the stock is heating, return the skillet to the stove. Heat 1 tablespoon olive oil over medium-high heat. Add the minced garlic and sauté until it softens, about 1 minute. Add the arborio rice and stir to coat it with oil. Add the wine and let it cook off for 30 seconds or until it is almost completely absorbed. Add 1 cup chicken stock and stir. Let the rice simmer until the stock is absorbed, stirring frequently. Add another cup of the chicken stock, stir, and let the liquid fully absorb. Continue adding the stock, a cup at a time and stirring frequently, until all of the stock is used and the rice is soft, about 20 minutes. Remove the rice from the heat, and stir in the margarine. Fold in the cooked squash and the dried sage. Serve immediately.

4. Leftovers may be refrigerated in an airtight container for up to three days or used for risotto cakes following the instructions above.

Salmon Croquettes

OK, I get it. Salmon croquettes have a bad rap all around. I remember what they used to taste like, but the flavors of the sweet potatoes and the salmon perfectly complement each other in these croquettes. The addition of the crushed cereal makes them nice and crispy. Considering that they are a great way to use up leftovers and that paired with a green salad they are a complete meal, you have a hit. **Serves 4**

2 cups gluten-, dairy-, soy-, nut-, and egg-free crisped rice cereal (I like Erewhon)

1 pound peeled sweet potatoes (about 4 small), cut into 1-inch cubes, or 1 (15-ounce) can sweet potato puree

1/4 teaspoon cayenne pepper

1 teaspoon salt

2 teaspoons lime zest

2 teaspoons cornstarch

12 ounces canned skinless, boneless salmon or leftover Poached Salmon (p. 34)

2 tablespoons finely chopped fresh chives

2 tablespoons olive oil

1. Place the cereal in a ziplock bag and seal it. Go over the bag with a rolling pin several times to crush the cereal into coarse crumbs. Pour the crushed cereal into a large, shallow bowl. Set aside.

2. If you are using fresh sweet potatoes, place them in a large saucepan and cover with water. Bring the water to a boil and cook the potatoes until they are tender, about 12–15 minutes. Pour the potatoes into a colander and drain them well. Return them to the cooking pot and mash them with a hand masher.

3. In a separate small bowl, combine the cayenne, salt, lime zest, and cornstarch.

4. Mix the salmon into the mashed sweet potatoes and then stir in the cayenne-salt mixture. Fold in the chives.

5. Scoop out 1/4–1/3 cup of the fish mixture and pat it into a cake to make about 8 patties. Carefully coat the outside of the cake with the crushed cereal. When all of the patties have been formed and coated, heat the olive oil over medium-high heat in a large, non-stick skillet. When the oil is hot, place the croquettes in the skillet and fry them 4 minutes per side, turning only once.

6. Remove the croquettes to plates and serve immediately.

7. Leftovers may be refrigerated in airtight containers for up to three days.

Note: Today there is a lot of concern about BPA-free cans. Please see the Where to Shop section (p. 182) for tips on where to get canned salmon that has little to no BPA.

Short Ribs

"Succulent and falling apart" are the words that I would use to describe these simple short ribs. I love to serve this dish over my Soft Polenta (p. 108) or my Potato and Celery Root Smash (p. 98).
SERVES 4

1. Place the vegetables in a 5-quart slow cooker and toss them with the cornstarch and salt to coat. Place the short ribs on top of the vegetables.

2. In a bowl, whisk together the balsamic vinegar and the beef stock. Pour this mixture over the top of the short ribs.

3. Cover the slow cooker and cook on low heat for 9 hours or until the meat is tender and falling apart. Serve immediately.

4. Leftovers may be refrigerated in an airtight container for up to five days.

2 small yellow onions (about 10 ounces), cut in wedges

1½ cups peeled and sliced carrots (about 10 ounces)

1½ cups sliced celery (about 6 ounces)

1 tablespoon cornstarch

1 teaspoon salt

3 pounds boneless beef short ribs

1 tablespoon balsamic vinegar

1 cup gluten-, dairy-, soy-, nut-, and egg-free beef stock (see Where to Shop, p. 182)

Snickerdoodle Muffins

I know that muffins really shouldn't be a main course, but I put them in this section because, while growing up, my mother never made muffins for breakfast. I love them for breakfast! I make a point of making muffins in the morning because I really like to dunk mine in coffee. A personal favorite, these muffins remind me of the snickerdoodle cookies that my grandmother used to make if she knew that we were dropping by. These are one step better, in my opinion. As I prefer a cake (and always a pound cake) to a cookie, I combined the two and came up with the perfect coffee companion. Not feeling like cinnamon? No problem. Omit the sugar and cinnamon coating and fold in diced fruit or berries instead. **MAKES 12 MUFFINS**

Canola oil
$1^1/_3$ cups superfine rice flour
$^1/_2$ cup potato starch
$^1/_4$ cup sorghum flour
1 cup sugar, divided
1 tablespoon baking powder
1 teaspoon xanthan gum
$^1/_2$ teaspoon baking soda
$^1/_2$ teaspoon salt
$^1/_4$ cup liquid unrefined coconut oil
1 cup cultured coconut milk, at room temperature (see Where to Shop, p. 182)
1 teaspoon vanilla extract
$^1/_4$ cup unsweetened applesauce, at room temperature
1 teaspoon ground cinnamon

Note: I like using unrefined coconut oil in this recipe because the coconut flavor lends a buttery flavor to the muffins, but if you do not like the coconut flavor, use refined coconut oil instead.

1. Preheat the oven to 375°F and grease (do not line) twelve muffin cups with canola oil.

2. In a large mixing bowl, whisk together the superfine rice flour, potato starch, sorghum flour, $^1/_2$ cup sugar, baking powder, xanthan gum, baking soda, and salt.

3. In another large bowl, mix together the liquid coconut oil, cultured coconut milk, vanilla extract, and applesauce. Mix the liquid ingredients until they are smooth.

4. Make a well in the center of the dry ingredients and pour in the wet ingredients all at once. Stir the batter until all of the ingredients are thoroughly incorporated.

5. Pour the batter into the prepared muffin tins and bake in the preheated oven for 14 minutes or until a toothpick inserted in the center comes out clean. Remove the tins from the oven and let the muffins rest in the tins for 10–12 minutes or until they are cool enough to handle but still warm.

6. While the muffins are cooling, stir together the remaining $^1/_2$ cup sugar and the ground cinnamon in a wide but shallow bowl.

7. When the muffins are cool enough to handle, roll each muffin in the cinnamon and sugar mixture until they are completely covered on all sides. Transfer the muffins to a wire rack to cool slightly and then serve warm, immediately, or let them cool completely.

8. Leftovers may be stored at room temperature in an airtight container for up to a day.

Stewed Fruit

I know that stewed fruit isn't one of the sexiest dishes around, but I have to tell you that one of the best things I've ever tasted in my life was a fresh date. I've only been lucky enough to have three fresh dates in my life, and since they are scarcely available in New York City, I have had to improvise. Craving juicy, fresh dates awhile back, I decided to reconstitute some of my favorite dried fruits and spice them up with cloves and cinnamon. Stewed fruit makes a delicious breakfast served with dairy-free Greek yogurt, especially in the wintertime when fresh fruit isn't as abundant. I developed this recipe before I had a serious reaction to figs last summer, so even though I omit the figlets these days, I left them in for you because they taste so good! **SERVES 4**

½ cup dried apricots
½ cup dried figlets (optional)
½ cup small, pitted prunes
¾ cup golden raisins
1 whole cinnamon stick
2 whole cloves
2¼ cups boiling water

1. Place the dried fruit in a large, heatproof bowl along with the cinnamon stick and cloves. Cover them with boiling water. Wrap the bowl tightly with plastic.

2. Let the fruit sit at room temperature for 2 hours and then place the container in the refrigerator to chill overnight. Serve with dairy-free Greek yogurt for breakfast, have it as a snack, or spoon it over dairy-free ice cream for dessert.

Note: This is also delicious served for breakfast or dessert with Indian Rice Pudding (p. 9).

Lettuce-Wrapped Herbed Turkey Burgers

My daughter Colombe is crazy for turkey burgers. If I'd let her, she would eat exclusively turkey burgers with a side of yams for every meal. Being a stubborn, but adorable, girl, I end up accommodating her turkey burger obsession, but the rest of the family gets tired of plain old patties after a while. So I pondered the turkey burger conundrum. How could I make one meal that everyone would enjoy? My husband and I needed to feel like we were eating a grown-up, filling meal, and the kids needed to feel like they were eating kid food while getting added nutrition. And then, as is often the case, I opened the fridge to see what we needed to use up. Of course, we had tons of leftover herbs and a head of Bibb lettuce, and I was reminded of my favorite restaurant when I was in high school. It was called the Vine Street Market, and it served the best turkey sandwich with herbs that I have ever tasted. Their version mixed the herbs into mayonnaise, which I can no longer eat, so I just blended them directly into the ground turkey. Do not feel limited by my herb suggestions. Sometimes I add some tarragon or cilantro to the mix. I truly use whatever is in the fridge, and the burgers are delicious every time. **SERVES 4**

1. Place the ground turkey in a large mixing bowl and add the chopped herbs, garlic, salt, and pepper. Thoroughly mix the meat with the herbs, garlic, salt, and pepper. I like to use my hands to make sure that everything is evenly incorporated. Form the meat and herb mixture into four patties.

2. Heat a lightly oiled grill pan or heat a lightly oiled gas grill over medium-high heat and add the turkey burgers. Cook for 6–7 minutes per side or until a meat thermometer inserted in the burgers registers 165°F. Since turkey burgers can dry out, do not press down on them with a spatula while cooking.

3. Remove the burgers from the heat. Place one burger in the center of each lettuce leaf and garnish with tomato slices. Wrap the lettuce around the burger and serve. Uneaten turkey burgers may be refrigerated in an airtight container for up to three days.

1 pound ground turkey
2 heaping tablespoons chopped mixed herbs (I use chives, dill, and Italian parsley, and sometimes tarragon, too)
1 clove garlic, finely minced
1/4 teaspoon salt
Dash of pepper
Oil for oiling the grill pan or grill grates
4 large Bibb or iceberg lettuce leaves
Tomato slices for serving (optional)

Note: A great way to store unused washed lettuce leaves is between damp paper towels in a sealed ziplock bag.

Note: It is possible to save leftover herbs by freezing them. Place washed and dried herbs in a single layer on a tray or baking sheet in the freezer. When they are frozen, transfer the herbs to airtight storage containers or bags; they will not stick together when frozen this way.

Ten-Minute Soba Salad

Sometimes I need to make a side that goes with the leftover chicken in the refrigerator, and this recipe always fits the bill. I always have some soba in the cupboard and cilantro in the fridge, so we eat this dish for dinner quite often. The buckwheat is such a nice change of pace from bland pasta, and I love the crunchy freshness of the sliced scallion and fresh cilantro. Make sure that when you buy soba noodles you get a brand that is made from 100 percent buckwheat; not all of them are. See the Where to Shop guide (p. 182) for brand recommendations. SERVES 4

1 (8-ounce) package
  buckwheat soba noodles
¼ cup rice vinegar
¼ cup canola oil
1 tablespoon sesame oil
½ teaspoon salt
1 scallion, dark green part
  only, thinly sliced (about 1
  tablespoon)
½ cup loosely packed cilantro
  leaves, chopped

1. Bring a large pot of water to a full, rolling boil. Add the soba noodles to the boiling water, stir, and boil for 8 minutes or until they are tender. Drain the noodles in a colander and rinse well with cold water until they are cool.

2. Meanwhile, whisk together the rice vinegar, canola oil, sesame oil, and salt to make a vinaigrette. Set aside. Transfer the noodles to a serving bowl and toss with the sesame oil vinaigrette. Stir in the scallion and cilantro. Serve immediately.

3. Leftovers may be refrigerated in an airtight container for up to three days.

Note: The key to cooking soba noodles is to prepare them in a large pot. If the pot is too small and the noodles are crowded, they will clump and form a mass of pasta that will not make a very nice salad. Trust me.

Tomato Caper Pasta Toss

I don't make a lot of pasta, but when I do, I like to load it up with chunky vegetables that add lots of color and flavor. Because I make this with grape tomatoes, and the olives and capers come in jars, this is a year-round favorite. I use green olives, but feel free to use whatever variety you prefer. **Serves 4**

1/4 cup plus 1 tablespoon olive oil

1 pound gluten-free spaghetti or angel hair pasta

1 pint grape tomatoes, quartered

3 tablespoons small capers

3 tablespoons chopped green olives (not pimento stuffed)

1/4 cup diced red onion

2 tablespoons lemon juice

1. Bring a large pot filled with water and 1 tablespoon olive oil to a rapid boil. Add the pasta and cook according to the instructions on the box.

2. While the pasta is cooking, mix together the tomatoes, capers, olives, red onion, lemon juice, and 1/4 cup olive oil in a large, heat-proof serving dish.

3. When the pasta is finished cooking, remove it from the heat and drain it in a colander. Toss the drained pasta with the tomato mixture and serve immediately.

Waffles

Whenever I make waffles, I think of my grandmother. Granny was not the best cook, but she loved parties. She told me once that during the Depression, just after she had married my grandfather, she wanted to have friends over for dinner and to play a game of bridge. Apparently, waffles were her forte, so she planned to serve breakfast for dinner, but in her nervousness, she forgot to grease the waffle iron, and the waffles stuck. Dinner was ruined. We always got a good laugh out of this story. She said she just served cocktails for dinner instead! Fast forward to my first "nonstick" waffle iron just a year ago: I followed the manufacturer's instructions to the letter, and sure enough, my first waffle stuck. My girls had a good laugh at my expense. Granny probably did, too. Now I remember to lightly grease the iron before each waffle goes in; just a brush of canola or grapeseed oil does the trick. While I do think that these are best hot off the griddle, I like to make a batch of these on the weekend and freeze them to eat throughout the week. Just pop the frozen waffles in the toaster for a minute or so to crisp them up. I cut them into triangles for the girls—sometimes half a waffle is enough for a weekday breakfast; we can even take them to go.
MAKES 6 LARGE WAFFLES

1⅓ cups superfine rice flour
½ cup potato starch
¼ cup sorghum flour
1 teaspoon xanthan gum
1 tablespoon baking powder
½ teaspoon baking soda
¼ teaspoon salt
2 tablespoons sugar
½ cup unsweetened
   applesauce
1½ teaspoons vanilla extract
⅓ cup canola oil
1¾ cups water
1 tablespoon cider vinegar
Syrup, confectioners' sugar,
   berries, and/or chocolate
   chips for serving

1. Preheat the waffle iron according to the manufacturer's directions. (I use a Cuisinart waffle iron on the #5 setting.)

2. In a large mixing bowl, whisk together the rice flour, potato starch, sorghum flour, xanthan gum, baking powder, baking soda, salt, and sugar. In a separate small bowl, whisk together the applesauce, vanilla extract, canola oil, water, and cider vinegar.

3. Pour the liquid ingredients into the dry ingredients, and mix them until all of the dry bits have disappeared, but there are still some lumps in the batter. When the waffle iron is ready, pour ⅔ cup batter onto the preheated waffle iron, spread to about ½ inch from the edge, close the top of the iron, and cook until the timer sounds or the waffle is done. Carefully remove the waffle from the iron onto a plate. Top with syrup or your desired toppings.

4. Freeze leftover, fully cooled, plain waffles between squares of waxed paper in airtight containers for up to three months. Remove from the freezer and toast in the toaster for a minute when you are ready to eat them.

Note: For an extra-special treat, eat these waffles the French way. Dip one side of a finished waffle in ½ cup melted gluten-, dairy-, soy-, nut-, and egg-free mini chocolate chips. Repeat until all six waffles have one side coated. Let them set, chocolate side up, on a wire rack until the chocolate is dry.

Warm Chickpea Salad with Cilantro and Lemon

I like when just a handful of ingredients can be thrown together into a delicious dinner for under ten dollars. This dinner can also be on the table in about 10 minutes, which makes me like it even more. Toss this together and then serve it family style over a big bowl of fluffy white rice. Dinner perfection. SERVES 4

1 tablespoon olive oil
¼ cup chopped onion (about
   ½ small onion)
2 (19-ounce) cans chickpeas,
   rinsed and drained
½ teaspoon salt
½ cup chopped cilantro leaves
2 tablespoons lemon juice
Rice for serving (optional)

1. Heat the olive oil in a large skillet over medium-high heat. Add the onions and reduce the heat to medium. Cook the onions for 5–7 minutes or until they are soft and translucent. Add the drained chickpeas and continue cooking for another 2–3 minutes, stirring frequently, or until the chickpeas are warmed through. Stir in the salt.

2. Remove the chickpeas from the heat and stir in the cilantro and lemon juice. Serve immediately over rice if desired.

3. The leftovers may be refrigerated in an airtight container for up to five days.

Watercress Salad with Flank Steak and Roasted Red Peppers

I serve this at least once a week for dinner, sometimes more often when it's hot out and I don't feel like cooking. Often I'll broil the steak over the weekend and have it ready in the refrigerator for a cold lunch during the week, too. I love the bitterness of the watercress combined with the spicy freshness of the chimichurri. The best part is that watercress is a natural diuretic, so I love to dig in to this one if I'm feeling a little bloated! My husband calls this one "Meat Salad," and it is one of our staples. It is inspired by my favorite salad at a New York City restaurant called Landmarc. **SERVES 4**

1 pound flank steak
Salt and pepper to taste
3 bunches watercress (about 5 ounces), washed and chopped
1 (7-ounce) jar roasted red peppers, drained and diced
1 recipe Chimichurri (p. 118)

1. Preheat the broiler. Place the flank steak on a rimmed baking sheet and sprinkle with salt and pepper. When the broiler is pre-heated, place the steak underneath, 4 inches away, for 7 minutes. Remove the steak from the oven, flip it, and return it to the broiler for another 4–5 minutes for medium-rare steak. Remove the steak from the oven and let it rest, uncovered, for 10 minutes before slicing thinly against the grain.

2. While the meat is resting, place the chopped watercress in a large salad bowl. Add the diced red peppers and Chimichurri and toss until ingredients are evenly distributed.

3. Divide the salad among four plates. Arrange slices of the thinly sliced steak on top of each plate of salad and serve immediately.

Wiener Schnitzel

OK, so the name itself gives away the fact that this is actually an Austrian, or rather, a Viennese dish. However, I think that most people probably associate it with all things German. So, while you could easily grill up some gluten-free wurst or sausages to serve at your backyard *Biergarten,* I like to fry up some crispy schnitzel instead. Because veal is actually the only meat that my oldest daughter asks for, I make this frequently. The key is to keep the oil temperature at exactly 350°F. If the oil gets too cold, the breading will fall off, and if it gets too hot, the breading will burn. But, if you use a thermometer and get the temperature just right, this schnitzel will make you feel like you are in a *Biergarten,* even on a Tuesday night. I like this schnitzel best served with Chunky Applesauce (p. 72) and my Mustard and Thyme Mash (p. 94). **Serves 4**

1. Place the veal cutlets in a single layer between two very long sheets of waxed paper. Pound the cutlets to 1/4-inch thickness all over to ensure quick and even cooking. (You can skip this step by asking the butcher to do it for you; he usually will.)

2. Pour the cultured coconut milk into one large shallow bowl. In another large shallow bowl, whisk together the corn flour, salt, and freshly ground pepper. Set both bowls aside.

3. Pour enough oil into a deep skillet so that it goes 1/4 inch up the sides of the pan. Heat the oil over medium-high heat until a candy thermometer in the oil measures 350°F.

4. While the oil is heating, coat each pounded veal cutlet with cultured coconut milk, letting the additional coconut milk run off. Then lightly dredge both sides of the cutlets with the corn flour mixture. Working in batches so you do not overcrowd the skillet, place the breaded cutlets directly into the hot oil and let them fry for 3 minutes total, turning once with tongs, being careful not to dislodge the coating. Remove the cooked schnitzel to a plate and continue adding cutlets, adding more oil between batches if necessary, until all of the veal is cooked. Serve immediately.

5. Schnitzel that is not served right away will not stay crunchy, but the leftovers may be refrigerated in an airtight container for up to three days.

Parchment paper
1 pound veal cutlets
3/4 cup plain cultured coconut milk (see Where to Shop, p. 182)
1 cup corn flour
3/4 teaspoon salt
1/4 teaspoon freshly ground pepper
Canola oil for frying
Candy thermometer

Note: If you buy your meat in the supermarket, sometimes you can find veal scallopini, which is veal cutlet already pounded thin. Otherwise, I just ask the butcher to pound the meat for me to save time.

sides

Variety is the spice of life, which is why side dishes are so important. I can eat chicken day after day, for example, as long as the side dishes that come along with it change frequently. Side dishes add color, texture, and unexpected flavors to our family favorites. I think of side dishes as dinner's accessories. If you have one or two reliable main courses and change up the sides, meals will never be boring.

Baked Plantains

I had never heard of a plantain until I moved to the Upper West Side, and I wasn't brave enough to taste one until my husband took me to Flor de Mayo on Amsterdam Avenue shortly after we met. I was not yet diagnosed with food allergies, and eager to please my new boyfriend, I acquiesced to trying this fried plantain thing that he suggested as a side with roasted chicken and black beans with rice. He was right. Fried plantains are delicious! The yellow plantains, that is. I'm not a huge fan of the green ones because they aren't as sweet. There are, however, two problems with fried plantains. Well, really three problems if you count the fact that once I start eating them, I cannot stop. The first problem is that, for people with food allergies, the fryer at a restaurant is an allergic reaction waiting to happen. Foods are not segregated before going in: The plantains go in after the breaded chicken fingers and so on. This is a problem for me since I can't have wheat. The second problem is that fried food isn't particularly healthy. Even though my palate wants it every night, my hips vehemently disagree. So does my heart. Consequently, when a friend with Latino roots told me his mother's recipe for baked plantains, well, I was all over it. Thanks to my friend Rick, plantains are not only the least labor-intensive side dish, but they are also one of the most delicious, and they're pretty healthy, too. **SERVES 4**

4 ripe sweet plantains (with black spots but not 100 percent black), about 12 ounces each

1 tablespoon soy- and dairy-free margarine (see Where to Shop, p. 182)

Pinch of salt (optional)

1. Preheat the oven to 350°F. With a sharp knife, slice the ends off of each plantain and then vertically score one side of each from tip to tip. Do not open the plantain; just slit it to allow steam to escape.

2. Wrap each plantain tightly in aluminum foil and place them on a baking sheet. Put the baking sheet in the preheated oven and bake the plantains for 40 minutes. Carefully unwrap the plantains, remove the peel, slice them, and place them in a serving dish. Toss with margarine and salt, if using. Serve immediately.

Baked Sweet Potato Fries

'Round our house, yams or sweet potatoes are on the menu almost every day. Sometimes I just bake them in the skins. Other times I'll dice them and put them in a breakfast hash with corned beef left over from the night before. At the end of the day, I'm a mom with small kids, so french fries are still a favorite. My girls beg for fries, and I feel good about giving them sweet potatoes. They are higher in vitamin A, C, and fiber than regular potatoes and, when baked rather than fried, they are much lower in artery-clogging fat. SERVES 4

2 pounds sweet potatoes or
    yams, peeled (about 3 large)
2 tablespoons olive oil
1 teaspoon coarse salt

1. Preheat the oven to 400°F.

2. Cut the potatoes lengthwise into fifths. Turn the potatoes on their sides and vertically slice them into fifths again, which should yield the usual french fry shape. If the fries are still too wide, halve them.

3. Dump the cut fries onto an unlined rimmed baking sheet and drizzle them with olive oil. Use your hands to mix the potatoes until they are completely coated with the oil. Spread the potatoes out into a single layer. Sprinkle them with salt and bake for 40–45 minutes, flipping after 20 minutes and again after 35 minutes.

4. Serve immediately. Leftover fries will go limp if not eaten right away.

Black Bean Salsa

Chips and salsa are just an easy snack to have around and an equally easy thing to serve to guests who pop in for a surprise visit. This is such a simple salsa that takes almost no time to make. Though it can be served immediately, this salsa tastes best if it's allowed to steep overnight; this allows the flavors to intensify. Serve with my homemade corn chips from *The Complete Allergy-Free Comfort Foods Cookbook* for an extra treat. **MAKES 2¹/₂ CUPS**

1 (14.5-ounce) can no-salt-added diced tomatoes

1 (15-ounce) can black beans, rinsed and drained

1 (4-ounce) can diced mild green chiles, drained

2 whole scallions, thinly sliced

1 clove garlic, minced

1 tablespoon packed finely chopped cilantro leaves

¹/₂ teaspoon salt

1 teaspoon cider vinegar

Gluten-free corn chips for serving (optional)

1. Empty the tomatoes and their juice into a large, nonreactive mixing bowl and add the beans, chiles, scallions, garlic, cilantro, salt, and cider vinegar. Stir to evenly incorporate the flavors.

2. Pour the salsa into an airtight container or into a serving dish and cover. Refrigerate overnight before serving to allow the flavors to combine. Serve with corn chips if desired.

3. Leftover salsa may be refrigerated in an airtight container for up to five days.

Chickpea French Fries

In Marseilles, these are called *panisses*. In my kitchen, however, they are just Chickpea French Fries. I love an alternate option to french fries, and it's always nice to have another starch on our family's menu. These are really easy to make, I always have chickpea flour on hand, and the method is much like making polenta. Make sure to whisk in the chickpea flour slowly, about $1/4$ cup at a time, or it will clump. Lumpy Chickpea French Fries aren't quite as good as smooth ones. **MAKES ABOUT 50 THICK-CUT FRIES**

Canola oil for greasing the baking sheet and frying

5 cups water

$1/2$ teaspoon salt, plus more for serving

$2^{1}/_{2}$ cups chickpea (garbanzo) flour

1. Lightly grease a large, rimmed baking sheet with a little canola oil and set it aside.

2. Bring the water and salt to a rapid boil in a large saucepan. Whisk in the chickpea flour in a steady stream, $1/4$ cup at a time, incorporating completely before adding more, and then reduce the heat to medium. Continue stirring until the mixture is smooth. Cook over medium heat for about 8 minutes or until the mixture is very thick.

3. Pour the mixture into the prepared pan, smooth it with a knife or spatula, and set it aside to set for about 10–15 minutes. The batter should be $1/8$–$1/4$ inch thick.

4. Pour the canola oil into a large skillet until it goes about halfway up the sides and preheat it to 350°F, or you can use a fryer to ensure that the temperature remains steady if you prefer.

5. While the oil is preheating, cut the set chickpea batter into "fries." I like mine thicker, so I cut them like steak fries, but you can make them narrower if you prefer. Add the panisses, a few at a time so as not to overcrowd the pan. Fry for about 5–7 minutes (the panisses should be completely covered with the oil) or until they are golden brown. Remove to a paper towel–lined plate to drain. Continue working in batches until all of the panisses are fried. Sprinkle with additional salt and serve immediately.

Chunky Cranberry Sauce

This lickety-split sauce is the cranberry sauce that I dreamed of as a child. I always found that the cranberry relish my grandmother contributed to our Thanksgiving dinner was too tart. This dish does not need to be reserved for Thanksgiving however. Keep it in the fridge year-round to serve on turkey sandwiches that need a little zip. **MAKES 2½ CUPS**

1. Combine the orange juice and sugar in a large saucepan over medium-high heat and bring to a boil, stirring constantly to dissolve the sugar.

2. Add the cranberries, raisins, cinnamon, and cloves. Reduce the heat and stir to thoroughly combine the ingredients. Simmer for 10 minutes or until most of the cranberries have burst and the sauce begins to thicken.

3. Remove the cranberry sauce from the heat and stir in the orange zest. Pour the cranberry sauce into a large, heatproof bowl. Refrigerate the sauce uncovered until it is completely cooled. Serve immediately, or cover and keep refrigerated until ready to serve for up to five days.

4. The leftovers may be refrigerated in an airtight container for up to five days.

1 cup orange juice
¾ cup granulated sugar
1 (12-ounce) bag fresh
  cranberries, picked over,
  washed, and drained
½ cup yellow raisins
½ teaspoon ground cinnamon
⅛ teaspoon ground cloves
Zest of 1 orange

Chunky Applesauce

Applesauce is one of my favorite snacks, and it's the perfect side to serve in early fall. After all, what could go better with sausage or Wiener Schnitzel (p. 61), Mustard and Thyme Mash (p. 94), and gluten-free beer? The chunkiness of this applesauce makes you feel like you're eating something of substance, and the sweet, cinnamony flavor offsets the saltiness and tanginess of the mustard and wurst. This is the perfect accompaniment to any Oktoberfest celebration, so get out your dirndl and dig in. And yes, I actually do have a dirndl. Serves 8

10 Gala apples (about 2½–3 pounds)
1 cinnamon stick
1½ cups water

1. Peel and core the apples and cut them into large chunks. Place the chunks in a large pot with the cinnamon stick and the water. Bring the water to a boil, reduce heat, and simmer for 15–20 minutes or until the apples are fork tender.

2. Remove the apples from the heat and reserve the cinnamon stick. Mash the apples by hand or with a potato masher until the apples form a chunky sauce. Place the applesauce in an airtight container, return the cinnamon stick to the applesauce, and let it chill completely before serving. Discard the cinnamon stick just before serving.

3. Leftovers may be refrigerated in an airtight container for up to a week.

Collard Greens

I never had much interest in collard greens. They are an awful lot like kale, and try as I might, I just am not that into kale. But when I found out that collards are really high in calcium, I decided to give them a try, and now I find them pretty irresistible. I prefer them cooked the Southern way, with bacon and in bacon fat, so this is a once-in-a-while side, but it really tastes good. I do not add any additional salt to mine because the bacon makes them so salty, but feel free to add salt to taste. SERVES **4**

4 strips bacon
¼ cup diced yellow onion
1 bunch collard greens (with
   center stems removed),
   washed, and chopped
2 teaspoons red wine vinegar

1. Place the bacon in a cold frying pan over medium-low heat. Cook the bacon for about 10–15 minutes, turning frequently, until it is crispy. Remove the bacon to a paper towel–lined plate to drain.

2. While the bacon is draining, pour off all but 1 tablespoon of the bacon fat—no need to wipe out the pan. Return the frying pan with the 1 tablespoon bacon fat to the stove and turn the heat to medium. Add the onions and cook until they are soft and translucent but not brown at the edges, about 5 minutes.

3. Add the collard greens and sauté them for about 5–7 minutes or until they are completely wilted and tender. Remove the collard greens from the heat and stir in the vinegar.

4. Crumble the bacon and stir it into the greens. Serve the collard greens immediately.

5. The leftovers may be refrigerated in an airtight container for three days.

Corn Quinoa Salad

If there is one recipe that I make more often than not in the summer, it's this one. This recipe came to me courtesy of Melissa Feldman, a writer who sometimes visits in the summer and who organized the most beautiful *Coastal Living* magazine photo shoot at our house a few years ago. We had so much fun having her and her crew as well as a bunch of our friends over for the dinner that the food stylists prepared. This was one of the recipes, and since that day it has moved to the front of my recipe box. Everyone always asks for the recipe once they have tasted it, so I thought that I would share it in this book. Thank you, Melissa! SERVES **6–8**

2 cups quinoa

4 cups water

2 teaspoons kosher salt, plus
 more to taste

3 cups fresh corn kernels (6
 ears)

1 bunch green onions, finely
 chopped (about 1 cup)

3/4 cup chopped fresh mint

1 tablespoon lemon zest

1/4 cup fresh lemon juice

1/4 cup extra-virgin olive oil

1/2 teaspoon freshly ground
 pepper

1. Rinse the quinoa very well in large sieve under cold running water for 5 minutes. Place 4 cups of water, the quinoa, and the salt in a large saucepan fitted with a lid and bring them to a boil, uncovered. Reduce the heat to a simmer, cover, and cook for 15 minutes or until almost tender. Drain the quinoa in a fine-mesh sieve and transfer it to a large serving bowl.

2. Combine the quinoa and the remaining ingredients. Mix the salad to distribute ingredients evenly, taste, and adjust the salt if necessary.

3. Refrigerate until the salad is completely chilled, about an hour, before serving.

4. Leftovers may be refrigerated in an airtight container for up to five days.

Recipe courtesy of Melissa Feldman, Stroll Productions

Corn Muffins

For years I missed out on corn bread, but when I wrote my first book, I developed a recipe for corn bread that I love. Over the years, I have made a few changes to improve upon perfection. It's also great that corn bread seems to be the quintessential kid recipe! If there is one thing that my kids have made more often than any other recipe in school, it's corn bread. Now the allergy sufferers in the classroom can take part, too. The kids will love getting in on the baking fun, and you'll love watching them have such a great time. **Makes 24 muffins**

24 paper cupcake liners
1⅓ cups superfine rice flour
¼ cup sorghum flour
½ cup granulated sugar
2 cups yellow cornmeal
½ cup potato starch
3 teaspoons baking powder
1 teaspoon baking soda
2 teaspoons salt
1¼ teaspoons xanthan gum
½ cup canola oil
2 tablespoons unsweetened
   applesauce
2 cups cultured coconut milk
   (see Where to Shop, p. 182)

1. Preheat the oven to 425°F and line twenty-four muffin tins with paper liners.

2. In a large bowl, mix together the flours, sugar, cornmeal, potato starch, baking powder, baking soda, salt, and xanthan until they are well combined.

3. In another bowl, whisk together canola oil, applesauce, and cultured coconut milk.

4. Pour the liquid ingredients into the dry ingredients, and stir until they are thoroughly incorporated and no dry pockets remain. Pour the batter into the prepared muffin tins.

5. Bake the muffins for 17 minutes or until golden and a toothpick inserted into the center comes out clean. Let the muffins cool for 5–10 minutes before turning them out onto a wire rack. Serve immediately.

6. These muffins are best served warm, but they may be stored in an airtight container at room temperature for up to three days.

Cranberry Chutney Jell-O Mold

Did your mom ever make Jell-O for dessert? Mine did, and I think that Jell-O molds, which were popularized in the 1950s, are a completely underappreciated side dish! What's not to love about a Jell-O mold? First, there's the Jell-O. Yum. And then there are all of the fruits that you can load up inside. Sometimes I need real comfort food, so I make a turkey breast and serve it with Mustard and Thyme Mash (p. 94), Roasted String Beans (p. 113), and this cranberry Jell-O mold for dessert. It feels just like Thanksgiving, even if we're eating it in July. I also love to bring this to potlucks because Jell-O molds are so unexpected these days, and everyone always loves them.

SERVES 6–8

1. Pour the cranberry Jell-O into a large, heatproof mixing bowl. Set aside.

2. Place 3½ cups water in a medium saucepan and add the cinnamon stick and cloves. Bring the water to a full boil and boil for 1 minute. Discard the cloves and the cinnamon stick.

3. Pour the boiling water into the Jell-O and stir until it is completely dissolved. Add the remaining 3½ cups cold water.

4. Transfer the bowl to the refrigerator to set for 2½–3 hours, or until the Jell-O is partially set but not completely solid. The texture will be like jelly. Stir in the raisins, diced apple, and orange zest.

5. Lightly grease the inside of a Jell-O mold or bundt pan with a little canola oil. Spoon the partially set Jell-O into the prepared mold and chill the Jell-O, uncovered, until it is completely set, at least 8 hours but up to overnight.

6. Invert the Jell-O mold on a platter lined with leaves of iceberg lettuce, if desired, and serve immediately.

7. Leftovers may be refrigerated in an airtight container for up to a week.

4 (0.3-ounce) packages cranberry Jell-O

7 cups cold water, divided

1 cinnamon stick

2 whole cloves

½ cup yellow raisins (about 3 ounces)

½ apple, peeled, cored, and finely diced (about 3 ounces)

Zest of 1 large orange (about 2 tablespoons)

Canola oil

Iceberg lettuce leaves for serving (optional)

Curried Cauliflower

I promised you inexpensive and easy, so here it is. I also promised you flavorful and delicious. Ditto. Have you ever noticed that cauliflower is super cheap at the store? As demand drives price, I'm betting that the demand is low—probably because everyone ate it boiled and flavorless as a child like I did. I am married to someone who hates cauliflower in every way but this one, and I see why. I think that roasting any vegetable can make it tasty, even the challenging ones, like brussels sprouts and cauliflower. Add the tanginess of curry powder, and this cauliflower is truly irresistible. **SERVES 4**

1 head cauliflower, broken into florets
2 tablespoons olive oil
1 teaspoon curry powder
½ teaspoon salt (or to taste)

1. Preheat the oven to 400°F.

2. Place the cauliflower florets in a large mixing bowl and add the olive oil, curry powder, and salt. Using your hands, mix to thoroughly coat the cauliflower with the oil and spices.

3. Dump the coated cauliflower onto a rimmed baking sheet and roast for 35–40 minutes or until the cauliflower is tender. Serve immediately.

4. Leftovers may be refrigerated in an airtight container for up to five days.

French Lentil Salad

A cold French lentil salad is one of my favorite things to eat on a hot day because it is refreshing yet filling. Lentils are really easy to make and taste great with just about everything. I make this simple recipe often and serve it as a side or put it over a green salad. It is delicious with sausage or chicken, but my favorite food to pair it with is cold Poached Salmon (p. 34). I think that this salad tastes best made with green Le Puy lentils, but they are a little bit more expensive, so feel free to use brown lentils instead. **Serves 4**

1 cup lentils (preferably Le Puy), rinsed and picked over

6 cups cold water

3 tablespoons red wine vinegar

1 tablespoon olive oil

½ teaspoon salt

1 tablespoon finely chopped shallot

¼ cup loosely packed Italian parsley leaves, finely chopped

1. Place the lentils and the water in a large saucepan and bring them to a boil. Reduce the heat to a simmer and cook the lentils for 15–18 minutes or until they are tender but not mushy. Pour the lentils into a colander, rinse well with cold water, and drain the lentils. When the lentils are cool, transfer them to a serving bowl.

2. In another small bowl, whisk together the red wine vinegar, olive oil, salt, and shallot to create a vinaigrette. Pour it over the lentils, toss to coat, and fold in the parsley. Serve immediately or loosely cover and place in the refrigerator to chill until ready to use.

3. Leftovers may be refrigerated in an airtight container for up to five days.

Gazpacho Salad

This light, colorful, and crispy salad is the perfect accompaniment to my Lettuce-Wrapped Herbed Turkey Burgers (p. 49). I find it really refreshing and love to have it for lunch with a piece of grilled chicken or fish, and thanks to delicious grape tomatoes, I can eat this salad year-round. My gazpacho salad has all of the elements of the traditionally cold Spanish soup, but I like that it's chunky, not pureed. **SERVES 4 GENEROUSLY**

1 pint grape tomatoes, quartered

1 pound unpeeled cucumber, diced (about 1–2 medium)

5 ounces diced orange or yellow bell pepper (about 1 small)

4 ounces diced red onion (about 1 small)

$^1/_4$ cup chopped Italian parsley leaves

1 tablespoon freshly squeezed lemon juice

$^1/_4$ cup olive oil

$^3/_4$ teaspoon salt

$^1/_4$ teaspoon sugar

1. Place the tomatoes, cucumber, pepper, red onion, and parsley in a large serving bowl and toss to evenly distribute the vegetables.

2. In a small bowl, whisk together the lemon juice, olive oil, salt, and sugar to create a vinaigrette and pour it over the salad. Toss to combine.

3. Serve immediately.

Note: To make this taste even more like traditional gazpacho, swap sherry vinegar for the lemon juice.

Grilled Asparagus

When I was a kid, my parents always grew asparagus in the garden, and I dreaded the day that they actually harvested it and made us eat it. Then sometime in my twenties, I stopped dreading asparagus and put it into frequent rotation on my weekly menu. I think what changed for me is that I started grilling rather than boiling it, and the little bit of char and added crispiness made me fall in love with this green vegetable. This grilled asparagus tastes especially good drizzled with my Simple Vinaigrette (p. 125). If you do not have a grill, do not despair: This is equally easy to make with a very hot stove-top grill pan. Serves 4

2 pounds washed asparagus
1 tablespoon olive oil
$^{1}/_{2}$ teaspoon salt

1. Preheat a gas grill or a grill pan to high.

2. Cut about 1 inch off the bottom of the asparagus stems. Place the trimmed asparagus on a rimmed baking sheet or platter and drizzle it with olive oil and salt. Using your hands, toss the asparagus until it is evenly coated with the oil and salt.

3. Using tongs, carefully place the asparagus on the grill, perpendicular to the grates. Reduce the heat to medium and cover the grill. Cook for 6 minutes and then turn the asparagus. Let it cook for another 6–7 minutes or until the asparagus is tender. Serve immediately.

4. Leftovers may be refrigerated in an airtight container for three to five days.

Guacamole

Since I grew up in Ohio, you might assume (correctly) that I didn't go into my backyard and pick avocados. Obviously, it's a place without avocado trees, and when I was a kid, avocados weren't as readily available in our neighborhood market as they are today. So, I spent at least a third of my life never having tasted an avocado and then at least another few years resisting friends' pleas to try one. It was green and smooshy. What can I say other than I just wasn't convinced? But one day, someone asked me to make some guacamole, and I took a lick. That was it, I was hooked. When I started developing the recipes for this book, I discovered that there are at least as many different ways to make guacamole as there are states in Mexico. So, I called my friend Jessica, who is Mexican, and asked for her input. She told me that she only puts salt and lime in hers. So, that's where I started. Then I threw in some cilantro and red onion just because I like them, garnished it with a spoonful of diced tomato, and voilà! We have guacamole. **MAKES 2 CUPS**

1 pound very ripe Haas avocados (about 2)

1 teaspoon freshly squeezed lime juice

1/4 teaspoon salt

1 tablespoon finely diced red onion

2 tablespoons chopped fresh cilantro leaves

1 tablespoon diced tomato for garnish (optional)

Gluten-free corn chips or vegetables for serving

1. Cut the avocados in half lengthwise and remove the peel and pits. Place the meat of the avocados in a large bowl. Add the lime juice and salt. Using a hand masher or the bottom of a plastic cup, mash the ingredients together until they are nearly smooth. Some lumps may remain.

2. Fold in the onion and cilantro and spoon the guacamole into a serving dish. Garnish with the tomato, if desired, and serve with gluten-free corn chips or sliced vegetables.

3. Guacamole is best eaten immediately, but leftovers may be refrigerated, with plastic wrap pressed directly onto the guacamole to prevent browning, for up to three days.

Note: You do not need a *molcajete,* or the Mexican stone bowl with a pestle in which guacamole is often made and served, to make guacamole. I find that the bottom of a sippy cup or other plastic cup works just as well to mash the avocado. Drop the avocado pit back into the finished guacamole and then press plastic wrap directly onto the guacamole to help prevent browning.

Note: An avocado is ripe when it is quite soft, but the skin does not feel as though it has separated from the flesh of the avocado.

Doughnut Holes

Do you know what kids like? Doughnuts. Do you know what parents like? Treats that aren't going to send their kids into a sugar-fueled orbit and that only require one bowl to prepare. These doughnut holes are so delicious served warm, and they met the approval of all the parents at school pickup the day that I tested them. Here's the funny part of the story: I forgot to add sugar to the dough when I was making it! So the only sugar in these little nuggets is the dusting that they get at the end. They are so yummy with just a hint of cinnamon. They are the perfect snack or Saturday morning treat with a cup of coffee. **Makes 24 doughnut holes**

1⅓ cups superfine rice flour

½ cup potato starch

⅓ cup sorghum flour

1 tablespoon baking powder

1 teaspoon salt

1 teaspoon xanthan gum

½ teaspoon cinnamon

½ cup unsweetened
   applesauce

¼ cup canola oil, plus more for
   frying

1 teaspoon vanilla

1 cup plus 2 tablespoons
   seltzer or club soda

½ cup granulated sugar for
   coating

1. Whisk together the superfine rice flour, potato starch, sorghum flour, baking powder, salt, xanthan gum, and cinnamon in a large mixing bowl.

2. In another bowl, whisk together the applesauce, ¼ cup canola oil, and vanilla extract, and set it aside.

3. Pour enough canola oil into a large, deep skillet or sauté pan to fill it about halfway up the sides, or fill a fryer according to the instructions. Heat the oil to 375°F, using a candy thermometer to gauge the temperature. If you are using a fryer, fill and heat it to 375°F according to the manufacturer's directions.

4. When the oil is hot enough, add the applesauce mixture to the dry ingredients and stir in the seltzer water. Stir until a smooth batter forms. Spoon the batter out a tablespoon at a time, roll it into smooth balls, and drop them into the hot oil. Fry each doughnut hole for about 8 minutes, flipping them after 4 minutes if they are not completely submerged in oil, or until they are completely golden and cooked through.

5. Using tongs, carefully remove the doughnut holes and transfer them to a paper towel–lined platter. While the doughnuts are draining, pour the sugar into a paper bag. Drop one or two of the warm doughnut holes into the bag at a time, and gently shake to coat them with sugar. Repeat this process until all the doughnut holes are fried and coated with sugar.

6. Serve immediately. These doughnuts are best eaten as soon as they are made, but they can be stored in an airtight container at room temperature for up to a day.

Herbed Biscuits

During college, before I was diagnosed with food allergies, I had the pleasure of tasting the biscuits at Red Lobster. They were awfully yummy, and I've always wanted to eat them again. This recipe creates a very close approximation. I am a biscuit snob, and spending time down South made me a real connoisseur. These biscuits are especially delicious split open and served piping hot with one of my Breakfast Sausage Patties (p. 5) in the center. What a tasty breakfast or wonderful weekend treat. The best part about these biscuits is that rolling out the dough is not necessary. Just drop them on the baking sheet, bake, and savor. **MAKES 8 BISCUITS**

1. Preheat the oven to 400°F.

2. In a large mixing bowl, whisk together the rice flour, potato starch, sorghum flour, xanthan gum, garlic salt, baking powder, baking soda, sugar, and fines herbes.

3. In another bowl, whisk together the cultured coconut milk, water, canola oil, and applesauce. Pour the liquid mixture into the dry ingredients all at once and stir until they are thoroughly combined and no dry bits remain.

4. Using a $1/2$-cup measuring cup, scoop out the dough and pat it into a ball. Place the ball on an ungreased baking sheet and bake the biscuits in the preheated oven for 20 minutes or until the biscuits are cooked through and just turning golden brown. Serve immediately.

2 cups superfine rice flour
$2/3$ cup potato starch
$1/3$ cup sorghum flour
$2^5/8$ teaspoons xanthan gum
1 teaspoon garlic salt
1 tablespoon baking powder
1 teaspoon baking soda
1 tablespoon granulated sugar
1 tablespoon dried fines herbes
1 cup cultured coconut milk
   (see Where to Shop, p. 182)
1 cup water
$1/3$ cup canola oil
$1/4$ cup unsweetened
   applesauce

Kale Salad with Chile Lime Vinaigrette and Sunflower Seeds

I can't lie. Until very recently I despised kale. I really mean that—I hated it. I roasted it time and time again, hoping that I could hop on the kale-chip bandwagon back when it was all the rage, but it just didn't happen. I spun it in the blender when I made smoothies. Oh, I drank them, but frankly, they were vile. However, my friend Lucy spent the summer in Bali awhile back, and when she came home on a raw diet, she finally introduced me to a way of eating kale that I could stomach. She showed me that dressed in a tangy, citrus vinaigrette, kale wilts a little, making it easier to chew. I discovered that a little heat in the form of pepper flakes and crunchiness thanks to the sunflower seeds makes this salad something I actually look forward to eating for lunch. Thanks to the newly available packages of washed and chopped kale, this recipe takes even less time to make and can be super colorful, too! SERVES 6

12 cups washed, stems removed, and shredded kale (about 14 ounces)

$1/4$ cup freshly squeezed lime juice

$1/4$ teaspoon red chile flakes (or more to taste)

$3/4$ teaspoon sugar

$1/2$ teaspoon ground cumin

$1/2$ teaspoon salt

$1/4$ cup canola oil

$1/4$ cup roasted, salted sunflower seeds (optional)

1. Place the kale in a large serving bowl.

2. In a small bowl, whisk together the lime juice, red chile flakes, sugar, cumin, and salt. Whisk in the canola oil to create a vinaigrette and immediately pour it over the shredded kale. Toss to coat completely. Sprinkle the salad with the sunflower seeds. Let sit 20 minutes to wilt slightly, or serve immediately.

3. Leftovers may be refrigerated in an airtight container for up to three days.

Mustard and Thyme Mash

Basically, this is just a smooth, creamy version of tangy German potato salad. Obviously, since I have several variations of mashed potatoes in this book, I never grow tired of a good mash. This one is simple and quick, but the mustard lends just the right zip to complement Wiener Schnitzel (p. 61) and Chunky Applesauce (p. 72). **Serves 4 generously**

1½ pounds Russet potatoes, peeled and cubed

¼ cup dairy- and soy-free margarine (see Where to Shop, p. 182)

¼ cup good-quality mustard (I use Maille)

½ teaspoon dried thyme

¼ teaspoon salt

1. Place the potatoes in a large pot and cover them with water. Bring the water to a boil and continue boiling for about 20 minutes until the potatoes are fork-tender. Remove them from the heat and drain.

2. Meanwhile, slowly heat the margarine until it is completely melted. Remove it from the heat and stir in the mustard, thyme, and salt.

3. Return the potatoes to the pot and turn the heat to high for 30 seconds to evaporate any remaining water. Turn off the heat. Add the margarine-mustard mixture and blend on low with a handheld mixer until the potatoes are completely smooth. Serve immediately.

4. Leftovers may be refrigerated in an airtight container for up to three days.

Naan

If you've never had naan, don't worry; I had never heard of it until a few years ago. Naan is an Indian flatbread that is always served in Indian restaurants. It's warm and soft, sort of a cross between a biscuit, a pancake, and bread. I love it. I prefer to make my version in a cast-iron skillet because it gets so hot, replicating a grill. A little char on the outside of your naan is a good thing—it lends authentic flavor. Sometimes I use the finished naan to make flatbread pizzas.

1$\frac{1}{3}$ cups superfine rice flour

$\frac{1}{3}$ cup plus 1 tablespoon
   potato starch

$\frac{1}{4}$ cup sorghum flour

$\frac{3}{4}$ teaspoon baking soda

$\frac{3}{4}$ teaspoon baking powder

$\frac{1}{2}$ teaspoon salt

2$\frac{5}{8}$ teaspoons xanthan gum

1 teaspoon sugar

1 tablespoon plus 1 teaspoon
   dairy- and soy-free
   margarine, melted (see
   Where to Shop, p. 182)

1 cup cultured coconut milk
   (see Where to Shop, p. 182)

$\frac{1}{4}$ cup water

Canola oil

1. Combine the superfine rice flour, potato starch, sorghum flour, baking soda, baking powder, salt, xanthan gum, and sugar in a large mixing bowl. Whisk well so that the dry ingredients are thoroughly combined.

2. In a small bowl, mix together the melted margarine, cultured coconut milk, and water. Add the wet ingredients all at once to the dry ingredients and stir until a dough forms and no dry bits remain.

3. Rub a cast-iron or nonstick skillet, or a nonstick griddle, with a little canola oil and then set over high heat for 2 minutes. While the skillet is heating, split the dough into four balls and work each ball into a disk, about $\frac{1}{4}$–$\frac{1}{2}$ inch thick and about 4 inches in diameter. (Traditional naan is made in an oval shape, but I find a circle easier to make.)

4. Place one naan in the skillet and reduce the heat to medium-high. Cook the first naan 2–3 minutes per side, until the outsides are golden brown in places or even a little charred and it is no longer doughy in the center. Continue with the remaining naan, though the cooking time may need to be reduced to 1–2 minutes per side if the skillet gets too hot. Serve the naan immediately as it tastes best hot off the griddle.

Potato and Celery Root Smash

Celery root is a pretty outstanding vegetable in my humble opinion. I always serve some form of celery root at Thanksgiving, and it always gets high marks, but don't reserve it just for the holidays! Although ugly before they are cooked, celery root has a tangy flavor and is lighter and less starchy than potatoes. The two combine beautifully into a fluffy mash that is anything but boring. The flavor is always an unexpected but welcome surprise, and this one is always a good conversation starter since celery root isn't the kind of vegetable that most people eat every day. Serve it with my Beef Tenderloin (p. 4), Brisket (p. 8), or a roast chicken. Serves 4

2 pounds Russet potatoes (about 2 large), peeled and cut into 1-inch pieces

1½ pounds celery root, trimmed, peeled, and cut into 1-inch pieces

1 teaspoon salt

¼ cup dairy- and soy-free margarine (see Where to Shop, p. 182)

1. Place the cubed potato and celery root in a large pot. Cover them with water and bring the water to a boil. Boil the potatoes and celery root, uncovered, for 20 minutes or until they are fork-tender.

2. Drain the vegetables in a colander, but do not rinse them, and return them to the cooking pot. Add the salt and margarine to the pot and, using a handheld electric mixer, whip the potatoes and celery root on medium speed until they are light and fluffy, about 2–3 minutes.

3. Leftovers may be refrigerated in an airtight container for three to five days.

Ratatouille

When it's hot outside, and I mean really hot, then two things are nearly certain: It's probably August, and tomatoes and zucchini are abundant. But to me, ratatouille is a cold-weather food. That's why I use canned, diced tomatoes in mine. I firmly believe that there is nothing better than a piping-hot bowl of ratatouille over white rice with a side of roast chicken to make me feel cozy on a cold winter's night. In my opinion, there is nothing more reminiscent of my year spent in France than this Provençal dish, and I love it so much that I have been known to cook up enormous batches and freeze them as a surprising side at Thanksgiving. Honestly, there's nothing like a bowl of ratatouille, and there's nothing like planning ahead! Serves **4**

1 tablespoon olive oil

2 cloves garlic, minced

$\frac{1}{2}$ cup diced yellow onion (about 3 ounces)

1 tablespoon red wine

1 cup diced zucchini (about 6 ounces)

1 cup diced eggplant (about 3 ounces)

1 (28-ounce) can diced tomatoes and juice

7 sprigs fresh thyme

1 bay leaf

1 teaspoon fines herbes or herbes de Provence

$\frac{1}{2}$ teaspoon salt

$\frac{3}{4}$ teaspoon granulated sugar

$\frac{1}{4}$ cup chopped Italian parsley

1. Heat the oil in a medium-size pot over medium-high heat. Add the garlic and onion and cook until they are soft, about 5–7 minutes. Add the red wine and let it cook off for about 30 seconds. Reduce the heat to medium, add the zucchini and eggplant, and sauté, stirring often, until they begin to soften, about 10–12 minutes. Add the tomatoes and their juice, thyme, bay leaf, fines herbes or herbes de Provence, salt, and sugar.

2. Simmer the ratatouille, covered, on low heat for 20 minutes, remove the lid, and continue simmering for an additional 10–12 minutes. The vegetables should be soft, and the sauce should have begun to thicken. Remove the thyme and the bay leaf, fold in the chopped parsley, and serve immediately.

3. Store leftovers refrigerated in an airtight container for up to three days. The completely cooled ratatouille may also be frozen in airtight containers for up to three months.

Kasha and Pasta

I am still trying to figure out exactly what the egg does in the traditional kasha *varnishkes* recipe. It's not a baked recipe, so it doesn't make it rise. Perhaps it is just there to add flavor and protein, though I am not sure. My recipe, because I am allergic to eggs, obviously doesn't contain any. I add flavor by cooking the buckwheat in chicken stock, though you can easily make this a vegetarian side by using vegetable stock instead. Le Veneziane (available online; see Where to Shop, p. 182) makes a close-enough gluten-free approximation to farfalle to stand in for the usual bowtie, but I prefer to use shells in mine because they are easier to come by and they look cute. Try this pilaf as a departure from the usual rice or potato side at dinner. SERVES 4–6

¾ cup corn-and-quinoa pasta (bowties or small shells)
2 tablespoons dairy- and soy-free margarine (see Where to Shop, p. 182)
½ cup diced onion
½ teaspoon salt
1 cup buckwheat groats
2 cups chicken stock

1. Bring a large pot of water to a boil. Add the pasta and cook it according to the package directions. Drain the pasta and set it aside.

2. Meanwhile, melt the margarine in a large saucepan over medium-high heat. When the margarine begins to bubble, add the onions and sauté them until they are soft, about 5 minutes. Stir in the salt.

3. Pour in the buckwheat and chicken stock and bring the mixture to a boil. Reduce the heat to a simmer and cover. Simmer for 10 minutes or until the stock is absorbed and the buckwheat is soft. Remove from the heat and stir in the pasta.

4. Transfer to a serving dish and serve immediately.

5. Leftovers may be refrigerated in an airtight container for up to three days.

"Refried" Beans

When I say that these beans are easy, I am not kidding. And, when I say that they are actually healthy, I'm also not kidding. These "refried" beans never get fried and do not contain lard. This vegetarian side only contains five ingredients (if you include the water), and though it takes a while in the slow cooker, it's so hands-off that you will have time to tend to other things, like filling up a piñata. **SERVES 4**

1. Place the pinto beans, onion, water, and salts in a 3-quart slow cooker. Cover and cook on high heat for 4 hours. The beans should be tender.

2. Spoon the contents of the slow cooker, including any remaining cooking liquid, into the bowl of a food processor and process until smooth. Serve immediately.

3. The leftovers may be refrigerated in an airtight container for up to three days.

½ **pound dried pinto beans**
½ **small yellow onion (about 3 ounces), peeled and cut in wedges**
3 **cups water**
½ **teaspoon salt**
¾ **teaspoon garlic salt**

Roasted Carrots

You have probably noticed by now that I really like to roast things, especially vegetables. This is because I love the way that vegetables taste when they are roasted rather than steamed. I used to shudder when my mother said that we were having glazed carrots. Gross. But then I tried roasted carrots, and cooked carrots no longer sounded unappealing. Delicately browned with a flavor similar to french fries, I find roasted vegetables hard to resist. I think you will, too. **SERVES 4–6**

2 pounds precut and peeled
   baby carrots, patted dry
   with paper towels
1 tablespoon plus 1 teaspoon
   olive oil
³/₄ teaspoon salt

1. Preheat the oven to 400°F.

2. Place the carrots in a large mixing bowl and toss with the oil and salt.

3. Arrange the carrots in a single layer on an unlined, rimmed baking sheet. Place the baking sheet in the middle of the preheated oven and roast for 50 minutes or until the carrots are fork-tender, stirring them twice to ensure even cooking. Serve immediately.

4. Leftovers may be refrigerated in an airtight container for up to three days.

Rösti

Traditionally Swiss farmer's food, rösti is one of my favorite ways to serve potatoes. Crispy and rustic, this easy two-step process is a beautiful way of bringing potatoes to the table: First, parboil the potatoes the day before so that they don't remain crunchy in your rösti—no one likes raw potatoes. Let them refrigerate overnight; the next day, grate them, and then cook them in hot margarine. Flipping this potato dish is actually the easiest part; do not be daunted. Just lay a platter or unrimmed baking sheet on top of the cooking pan, turn it out, and then slide it back in. This delicious potato cake just needs a few sprigs of thyme scattered around the bottom as garnish, and it is sure to become a dinner party or brunch showstopper. If you celebrate Hanukkah, this is the perfect latke alternative. In fact, this is the way that my husband's grandmother used to make potato pancakes. I find that cooking the rösti in Earth Balance dairy- and soy-free margarine provides enough salt, but feel free to sprinkle on a little extra before serving, if desired. **SERVES 6**

3 pounds Russet potatoes,
    peeled and cut in half
Salt to taste
¼ cup canola oil or dairy- and
    soy-free margarine, divided
    (see Where to Shop, p. 182)
Thyme sprigs for garnish

1. Place potatoes in a large pot and cover with water. Generously salt the water, place the pot on the stove, and turn heat to high. Bring the water to boil and boil the potatoes, uncovered, for 10–15 minutes or until they are soft but not completely cooked through.

2. Drain the potatoes, place them in a large covered container or bowl, and refrigerate overnight.

3. The next day, grate the potatoes and set them aside.

4. Add 2 tablespoons margarine to a 10-inch paella pan or cast-iron skillet, place on the stove, turn the burner to medium-high, and let margarine melt completely. When the margarine begins to bubble, add the grated potatoes. Using a spatula, press the potatoes down, forming a cake. Reduce heat to medium and let the potatoes cook, uncovered and undisturbed, for 15 minutes. Turn the heat back up to medium-high and cook for another 5 minutes. Run a knife or the spatula around the edges to loosen the potatoes. Place a platter on top of the pan, invert the rösti, and let it slide out onto the platter.

5. Add the remaining margarine to the pan. Heat it over medium-high until it bubbles. Swirl the pan to coat the sides with the margarine. Carefully slide the uncooked side of the rösti back into the pan. Cook for another 10 minutes on medium-high heat.

6. Run a knife around the edges again, place a platter on top of the pan, and turn out the rösti. Garnish with thyme sprigs and serve immediately.

7. This dish is best served right away but can be refrigerated in an airtight container for up to three days.

Soft Polenta

I love polenta, although it will always be grits to me. When I was diagnosed with wheat allergies, I quickly transitioned from pasta to polenta, and instead of Cream of Wheat, I started serving this for breakfast, too. I love polenta's versatility. What I only recently began to understand about polenta is that the key to its success is always "slow and steady wins the race." Pay close attention to these directions: Add the polenta to the boiling water ¼ cup at a time and cook the polenta over very low heat. Adding the cornmeal too quickly causes lumps, and cooking it over higher heat causes it to thicken too quickly, before it's ready. Whether you choose to serve it creamy or let it set up and slice it, it works with just about any dish. I particularly love it with Ratatouille (p. 100) or a chicken stew. I frankly can't think of anything much cozier to serve as a late fall or early winter side. SERVES 6

6 cups water

2 teaspoons salt

1¾ cups cornmeal

3 tablespoons dairy- and soy-free margarine (see Where to Shop, p. 182)

1. Bring the water to a boil in a large saucepan. When the water is boiling, slowly whisk in the cornmeal ¼ cup at a time, making sure that each addition is completely stirred in before adding the next ¼ cup. After all the cornmeal has been added, reduce the heat to low. Cook, stirring often, over low heat for 30 minutes. Remove the polenta from the heat and stir in the margarine.

2. Serve immediately for soft polenta or pour into a lightly oiled pizza pan for Polenta Pizza (p. 36).

3. Refrigerate leftovers in an airtight container for up to five days.

Roasted String Beans

One day my youngest daughter and I were in the supermarket, where she spent the entire trip begging for some potato-chippy snack things that were supposed to be like a fried vegetable. I suppose that the creators of these snacks hoped that parents would feel good about serving their kids a "vegetable" and would therefore buy the product. I figured that if she really wanted a crispy string bean, I'd make one for her. These are not exactly chips, but they are salty and healthier than that stuff that comes in a bag. My husband swears they taste like the string beans from a Chinese restaurant without the garlic sauce. I'm allergic to string beans so I can't eat these, but my children and husband (who are not allergic) have definitely given them their seals of approval. SERVES 4–6

1. Preheat the oven to 400°F. Place the string beans in a large bowl and sprinkle them with olive oil and salt. Using your hands, toss them together to evenly distribute the salt and oil. Dump the beans onto an unlined, rimmed baking sheet and arrange them in a single layer.

2. Roast the string beans in the preheated oven for 20 minutes. Taste and adjust the salt if necessary. Serve the prepared string beans immediately.

3. Leftovers may be refrigerated in an airtight container for up to three days.

$1\frac{1}{2}$ pounds string beans, trimmed
1 tablespoon olive oil
$\frac{1}{2}$ teaspoon salt

dressings and dippers

To me, every cook needs to have a good chicken recipe, a good vegetarian recipe, and one dessert recipe committed to memory, and he or she must also know how to make vinaigrette. Bottled vinaigrettes are convenient, but they are loaded with ingredients that our bodies don't need. Fresh vinaigrettes are exactly that: fresh. They are also flavorful and often aromatic. Vinaigrettes never take more than five minutes to create, and they make any salad more interesting, piquant, and enticing. This short section will give you some new ideas about how to "dress up" your salads and entrees.

Asian Dressing and Dipping Sauce

Coconut aminos is such a wonderful addition to the pantry for anyone allergic to soy but craving Asian food. I love the flavor combination and the versatility in this dressing. To me, a really good recipe is like a little black dress: You can pair it with just about everything. I keep a little of this dressing in the fridge to use in Bang Bang Chicken (p. 2) or as a rich, delicious dressing on a simple salad. It is also a tasty dipping-sauce alternative to plain old soy sauce when you're eating sushi. Of course, for this sauce/dressing, if you are serving it to children, you may want to reduce the amount of chile flakes. MAKES ¾ CUP

¼ cup tahini
¼ cup raw coconut aminos
2 tablespoons toasted sesame
  oil
2 tablespoons rice vinegar
¾ teaspoon red chile flakes

1. Whisk together all the ingredients in a bowl until they are smooth.

2. Leftovers may be refrigerated in an airtight container for up to one week.

Chimichurri

Chimichurri is a delicious herb sauce native to Argentina, but have you ever noticed that many countries have their own variation? In Italy it's called *salsa verde*. In Morocco it's called *charmoula*. Each is very similar to the other, but with a little twist. Salsa verde usually has anchovies in it, and charmoula contains cilantro. I like to make chimichurri and keep it around to serve over chicken, steak, fish, or salad. It is yummy on just about everything and makes a great marinade or vinaigrette.

MAKES ABOUT 2 CUPS

2 garlic cloves, minced
1 cup chopped Italian parsley
1 tablespoon chopped fresh
   oregano
$1/2$ teaspoon red chile flakes
$3/4$ teaspoon salt
1 teaspoon white wine vinegar
$3/4$ cup olive oil

1. Place all of the ingredients in a small bowl and mix together.

2. The chimichurri may be refrigerated in an airtight container for up to three days.

Note: Just a tablespoon or two of this goes a long way as a sauce for grilled meat or fish.

Green Curry Paste

Oh, wow, do I like green curry! It's hot, it's fresh, and it's generally served with rice and creamy coconut milk. What's not to like? I'm not really a big fan of the bottled green curry pastes. They aren't as fresh as I like, so I made this curry paste that is almost like a Thai pesto. It's similar to a curry sauce at Sang Lee, a farm stand on the North Fork of Long Island, and the inspiration for this recipe. This curry paste freezes beautifully, so I make it, press plastic wrap on top of it, and freeze it in an airtight container for the next time I'd like a chicken, shrimp, or veggie curry. I even use it as a tangy dip with raw vegetables. **MAKES 2 CUPS**

1 (14-inch) lemongrass stalk (about 2 ounces), chopped

1 (3-inch) piece peeled ginger (about 2 ounces)

6 ounces washed and dried fresh cilantro leaves and stems

1 ounce fresh mint leaves (about 1 cup)

1½ ounces fresh basil leaves (about 1½ cups)

1 shallot (about 1 ounce), quartered

5 cloves garlic

¼ cup freshly squeezed lime juice

¾ teaspoon sugar

1 (4-ounce) can diced mild green chiles

1½ teaspoons salt

¼ cup canola oil

1. Add the lemongrass, ginger, cilantro, mint leaves, basil leaves, shallot, garlic, lime juice, sugar, chiles, and salt to the bowl of a food processor. Puree for 2 minutes or until the ingredients are smooth.

2. With the processor on, add the canola oil in a steady stream and continue blending until the curry paste is completely smooth.

3. Use the curry paste immediately or freeze, with plastic wrap pressed down directly on top of the curry, in an airtight container for up to three months. Thaw completely before using.

Herbed "Butter"

When I lived in Chattanooga during high school, I had lunch at a restaurant called Vine Street every Saturday. This quirky little restaurant was part high-end food store and part cafe. It had a walk-up window and was wood paneled and dark, and it had the best sweet mint tea I've ever tasted. They also made a fruity chicken salad that was the inspiration for the chicken salad in *The Complete Allergy-Free Comfort Foods Cookbook*, but my favorite dish was a chive turkey sandwich served on a hamburger bun. It was slathered with mayo and dotted with minced chive and garlic. Today the eggs in the mayonnaise would cover me in a rash from head to toe, so I developed this spin on my favorite condiment just for spreading on toast or sandwiches. It is delicious on the Crusty White Bread from *The Complete Allergy-Free Comfort Foods Cookbook,* but you don't just have to stick to chives and garlic. You could swap Italian parsley, tarragon, or any other herb that you enjoy. **Makes 1 cup or 16 servings**

1 cup dairy- and soy-free margarine, softened but not melted (see Where to Shop, p. 182)
1 tablespoon plus 1 teaspoon chopped chives
1 clove garlic, minced

1. Place the softened margarine, chives, and garlic in a mixing bowl and stir them together to evenly distribute.

2. Spoon the margarine into a small serving bowl or lidded container and refrigerate until ready to use or for up to five days.

Note: For a fancier variation, the Herbed Butter may also be dropped by spoonfuls into a straight line down a sheet of parchment paper and rolled into a log. Tie the parchment paper at the ends and refrigerate the log for at least 2 hours. Slice pats like you would from a stick of butter.

Note: To jazz up a roast chicken or turkey, stuff spoonfuls of this herbed margarine between the breast and the skin before roasting. This is also delicious melted on flank steak hot off the grill or in a piping-hot baked potato.

Sherry Vinaigrette

How I went from despising salad to eating it at least once and sometimes twice a day I'll never know. I've been converted. I think it's because at a certain point, I realized that a variety of lettuces outside of the familiar iceberg exist. I love Bibb and red-leaf lettuce, but what I really love is a mélange of lettuces dressed with a light but flavorful homemade vinaigrette. Try mixing frisée (also known as curly endive), finely sliced endive, red-leaf lettuce, and a little mâche, all of which I find organic and prewashed at the supermarket, and then adding this delicious vinaigrette for the perfect salad. MAKES 1 CUP

¼ cup sherry vinegar
¾ cup olive oil
1 tablespoon finely diced
  shallot
1 teaspoon salt
¼ teaspoon freshly ground
  pepper

1. Whisk together all of the ingredients and pour ¼–½ cup over a large salad. Toss the salad to thoroughly coat it with vinaigrette. Add more if necessary. Serve the salad immediately.

2. Leftover vinaigrette may be covered and refrigerated for up to three days. Shake or whisk the vinaigrette thoroughly before using again.

Simple Vinaigrette

One day, I had two tweens over for a baking lesson, and I explained that there are a few recipes that everyone needs to have committed to memory. A simple vinaigrette is one of them. This recipe is delicious and versatile. It works on everything from a green salad to Cobb Salad (p. 18) to a tomato salad. I use it almost daily. **Makes about ³/₄ cup**

1. Place the minced shallot, Dijon mustard, white wine vinegar, and salt in a small bowl and mix them together with a small wire whisk. Continue whisking and add the oil in a steady stream. Continue until the dressing forms a thick emulsion.

2. Use immediately or cover and refrigerate for up to three days. Whisk again before using the leftovers.

2 teaspoons minced shallot
1 tablespoon good-quality Dijon mustard (I like Maille)
1 tablespoon white wine vinegar
¹/₄ teaspoon salt
¹/₂ cup olive oil

desserts

I did not get the memo about desserts being taboo. Nope, I didn't. I like dessert, and I believe that it has a place in every-day life, so I refuse to give it up. The problem for me is knowing when to say when. I love to indulge my sweet tooth, and I think it's important to do so. Why? Well, when I feel deprived, I overeat. So, I eat just a little dessert every day; it does wonders for my taste buds and my mood, and it gives me something to look forward to at the end of the day. I also like the idea of filling up the cookie jar with fresh cookies rather than packaged ones. Whether you like dessert every day or you prefer to indulge only once in a while, the mouthwatering desserts in this section will surely hit the spot, and some may even conjure wonderful childhood memories. Hopefully some of these recipes will inspire new memories, too.

Apple Crumble

I make this in the fall, using a couple of leftover vanilla cupcakes for the topping, and serve it with nondairy ice cream or whipped topping. It's the easiest thing to make, especially because I usually keep unfrosted cupcakes in the freezer, because you never know when you might want a quick treat or to use them for something else. The addition of the apple butter eliminates the step of adding spices. I prefer the Vermont Organics brand of apple butter because it is so cinnamony and clovey. SERVES 6–8

Crumble Topping

1½ cups crumbled unfrosted Basic Vanilla Cake (p. 134), about 2 cupcakes

2 tablespoons packed light brown sugar

¼ cup butter-flavored organic palm fruit oil shortening or dairy- and soy-free margarine (see Where to Shop, p. 182)

Apple Filling

3 pounds Granny Smith apples (about 6–8 large apples), peeled, quartered, and sliced, preferably on a mandolin, ⅛ inch thick

½ teaspoon salt

2 tablespoons butter-flavored organic palm fruit oil shortening or dairy- and soy-free margarine (see Where to Shop, p. 182)

1 tablespoon cornstarch

2 tablespoons cold water

¾ cup apple butter

½ cup raisins or dried cranberries

1. Preheat the oven to 350°F and lightly grease a 9-inch deep-dish pie plate.

2. Make the crumble topping by mixing together the crumbled cupcakes and the brown sugar. (I like to use my hands to work these two ingredients together because it is easy and ensures that the cupcakes get evenly coated with the sugar and shortening.) Cut in the butter-flavored shortening until clumps form. Place the crumble topping in the refrigerator until ready to use.

3. Toss together the apples and the salt in a large mixing bowl. Melt the shortening or margarine in a large skillet over medium-high heat. Add the sliced apples and sauté for about 3 minutes or until the apples begin to soften.

4. Meanwhile, in a small separate bowl, whisk together the cornstarch and water until they are smooth. Add the cornstarch mixture to the apples. Stir to evenly combine them. Continue cooking for another minute or until the cornstarch begins to thicken and the apples are soft.

5. Remove the apples from the heat and fold in the apple butter and the raisins or dried cranberries. Spoon the mixture into the prepared pie plate and top with the crumble topping.

6. Bake the apple crumble in the preheated oven for 40 minutes.

7. Remove from the oven and let the crumble cool. The crumble can be served warm or room temperature.

8. Leftovers may be refrigerated in an airtight container for up to three days.

Apricot Fool

Fool is a traditional British dessert that, in this case, takes maybe one minute and thirty seconds to make. I told you I wanted this book to be about quick and economical recipes! I was not kidding. Usually, a fool is just a mess of fruit sauce and whipped cream, so I used my coconut-milk Whipped Cream recipe (p. 181) and just stirred in a little apricot jam to make this super fast. You could serve this with a cookie or just spoon it into a parfait glass, whichever you prefer. I love this dessert because it is rich and creamy but fruity at the same time. It's perfect for summertime when you want something impressive for dessert but don't feel like standing at the stove for hours.
SERVES 4–6

4 (14-ounce) cans coconut milk, unshaken and refrigerated
1 teaspoon vanilla
3/4 cup apricot jam

1. Place a large metal mixing bowl, the metal beaters from a hand-held mixer, and the cans of coconut milk in the refrigerator for at least 1½ hours.

2. Remove the cans from the refrigerator, open, and skim the solid "cream" from the top of the each can of coconut milk and place it in the chilled metal bowl. *If the cream is not solid but still soft, return it to the refrigerator to chill until it is solid; otherwise this recipe will not work.* This should yield about 4 cups cream. Discard the remaining coconut water or reserve it for another use.

3. Add the vanilla extract to the chilled coconut solids and beat with a handheld mixer on medium speed for about 30 seconds or until the coconut solids are creamy and soft peaks form.

4. Fold in the apricot jam and spoon the fool into parfait cups or small bowls. Serve immediately. The whipped cream will soften considerably at room temperature so these really are best eaten right away.

Note: Do not feel as though this can only be made with apricot. It is delicious to fold any jam that you have on hand into the whipped cream.

Bark So Many Ways

At the holidays, do you find yourself up to your eyeballs in teachers' presents and gifts for neighbors, your hairdresser, the mailman, and your friends? I do! But, like me, you probably don't want to spend a fortune or devote an entire week to making perfectly decorated holiday cookies—so don't. Instead, try making bark a million different ways, and everyone will be touched by the fact that you made something just for them. Only you will know that it only took 5 minutes. This is a recipe that is really just a guideline. Once you get past melting the chocolate, let your imagination run wild with the toppings and the amounts. I never practice much restraint and load them on. I offer some topping suggestions, but get creative with your own! I'll bet you can come up with tons of really delicious combinations. SERVES **10–12**

For the Bark Base

Canola oil
2 pounds gluten-, dairy-,
  soy-, nut-, and egg-free
  semisweet chocolate chips

Topping Suggestions

Mini candy canes, crushed
Mini marshmallows
Crisped rice cereal
Crushed Enjoy Life Foods
  Crunchy Vanilla Honey
  Graham Cookies and
  marshmallows
Gluten-free pretzels
Chopped dried fruit, such as
  apricots, cherries, and/or
  raisins
Pepitas
Shredded, sweetened coconut
Popped popcorn

1. Very lightly grease two rimmed 9 x 12 x ½-inch baking sheets with a little canola oil. Set aside.

2. Place the chocolate chips in a large microwave-proof bowl. Microwave in 10- to 20-second intervals (about a total of 1 minute and 30 seconds) until the chocolate is two-thirds melted. Remove the chocolate from the microwave and stir until the chocolate is completely smooth. Pour the chocolate into the prepared pan and sprinkle with the toppings of your choice. Place the bark in the refrigerator to chill for at least 1 hour.

3. Cut or break the finished bark into pieces. Keep refrigerated until ready to serve.

4. Leftovers may be refrigerated in an airtight container for up to a week.

Note: If you can tolerate soy lecithin, try swapping the chocolate chips for vegan white chocolate chips. See the Where to Shop guide (p. 182) for suggestions.

Basic Vanilla Cake

Seriously, what is better than a slice of moist, delicious vanilla cake on a Saturday at 4:00 p.m.? Maybe a good cup of black coffee to go with it, but otherwise, I can't think of much else. While I was growing up, my grandfather came over every Saturday at four for a proper tea. It wasn't formal. It was more like the familial coffee klatch. He was known for his pound cake and often brought one with him. When he didn't bake, this former restaurateur expected my mother—his daughter—to make something fresh. My mom often made a vanilla cake with jam between the layers one week, a vanilla cake with chocolate frosting the next, and so on. You get my point. A vanilla cake yields a lot of different possibilities once you have a good recipe for one.

Here's how I came up with the idea to add cannellini beans for additional moisture: black bean brownies. Everyone always raves about how delicious black beans are in chocolate brownies, so why not white beans in vanilla cake? It works. Use this recipe as the foundation for so many of my other dessert recipes and then let your imagination run wild. **Makes 24 cupcakes, 1 9x13-inch rectangular cake, or 2 8-inch rounds**

24 paper cupcake liners
1 (15-ounce) can cannellini beans, rinsed and drained
2 cups superfine rice flour
$^2/_3$ cup potato starch
$^1/_3$ cup sorghum flour
1 tablespoon baking powder
$^1/_2$ teaspoon salt
1 teaspoon baking soda
1 teaspoon xanthan gum
$^1/_2$ cup organic palm fruit oil shortening (butter-flavored or plain)
2 cups granulated sugar
$^1/_2$ cup unsweetened applesauce
2 teaspoons vanilla extract
1 cup cultured coconut milk (see Where to Shop, p. 182)
1 recipe Even Easier "Buttercream" Frosting (p. 162, optional)

1. Preheat the oven to 350°F and line twenty-four cupcake tins with paper liners. (You can also lightly grease the bottom and sides of a 9 x 13-inch pan, two 8-inch round pans, or two 9-inch round pans instead.) Set them aside.

2. Place the rinsed and drained cannellini beans in the bowl of a food processor and process until they are completely smooth. Set them aside.

3. In a large mixing bowl, whisk together the superfine rice flour, potato starch, sorghum flour, baking powder, salt, baking soda, and xanthan gum. Set them aside.

4. In the bowl of a stand mixer, cream together the shortening and sugar for 2 minutes on medium-high speed or until they are light and fluffy.

5. Scrape down the sides and beat in the bean puree, the applesauce, and the vanilla extract. Scrape down the sides and then beat the mixture again on medium-high speed for another minute. Scrape down the sides.

6. Slowly stir in the dry ingredients and with the mixer on low, pour in the cultured coconut milk. Stir just until the batter is completely blended.

7. Pour the cake batter into the prepared cupcake tins and bake until a toothpick inserted in the center comes out clean. Cupcakes need to bake for about 22 minutes, a 9 x 13-inch cake takes about 30 minutes, 8-inch round cakes need about 30–35 minutes, and 9-inch round cakes take about 27 minutes. When the cakes are golden brown and a toothpick inserted in the center comes out clean, remove them from the oven.

8. Let the cakes cool in the pans for 15 minutes and then turn them out on a wire rack to cool completely before frosting.

9. Leftover frosted cake may be stored, tightly wrapped, at room temperature for up to three days. Completely cooled, unfrosted cake may be tightly wrapped and frozen for up to three months.

Blondies

Soft and chewy, thick and chocolaty, these are always a traditional crowd favorite. As a busy parent, I prefer to make blondies because they don't take as long as drop cookies. I don't know anyone who can resist these squares, and rarely do we have any leftovers. Pull up a glass of nondairy "milk" and dig in. **Makes 24 bars**

2¼ cups Bob's Red Mill Gluten-Free All-Purpose Baking Flour

1 teaspoon baking soda

1 teaspoon baking powder

⅝ teaspoon xanthan gum

1 teaspoon salt

1 cup organic palm fruit oil shortening (butter-flavored or plain)

1¼ cups light brown sugar

¼ cup granulated sugar

2 teaspoons vanilla extract

2 tablespoons ground flaxseed meal

6 tablespoons water

1 (10-ounce) bag of gluten-, dairy-, soy-, nut-, and egg-free chocolate chunks

1. Preheat the oven to 350°F and lightly grease a 9 x 13-inch baking pan.

2. Whisk together the flour, baking soda, baking powder, xanthan gum, and salt in a large mixing bowl.

3. In the bowl of a stand mixer, cream together the organic palm fruit oil shortening, brown sugar, and granulated sugar until they are fluffy. Scrape down the sides and beat in vanilla extract.

4. Mix together the flaxseed meal and the water in a separate bowl and add this mixture to the batter. Beat the batter until it is light and fluffy again. Scrape down the sides.

5. Slowly stir the dry ingredients into the wet ones and mix until the dough comes together and all the ingredients are evenly incorporated. Fold in the chocolate chunks.

6. Spread the batter into the prepared baking dish. Bake for 22–25 minutes or until the edges are just golden and the center is set. Let cool completely before cutting into squares.

7. Leftovers may be stored in an airtight container at room temperature for up to three days.

Apple Streusel Cake

Honestly, I just love this simple cake. I rarely wait for it to cool completely before eating it. It is so delicious with vanilla dairy-free ice cream and makes the perfect afternoon snack. I just have to remind myself that several slices of the cake are not equivalent to several slices of fruit! **Serves 8**

Streusel

⅓ cup superfine rice flour

¼ cup packed light brown sugar

¼ teaspoon xanthan gum

½ teaspoon ground cinnamon

2 tablespoons cold organic palm fruit oil shortening (butter-flavored or plain)

Cake

1 cup superfine rice flour

⅓ cup potato starch

3 tablespoons plus 1 teaspoon sorghum flour

1½ teaspoons baking powder

½ teaspoon baking soda

½ teaspoon xanthan gum

¾ cup sugar

¼ cup butter-flavored or plain organic palm fruit oil shortening

¼ cup applesauce

½ cup cultured coconut milk (see Where to Shop, p. 182)

½ medium red apple (4 ounces), peeled, cored, and diced

1. Preheat the oven to 350°F and grease a 9 x 5-inch loaf pan.

2. Make the streusel topping by whisking together the superfine rice flour, sugar, xanthan gum, and cinnamon. Cut in the palm fruit oil shortening just until large clumps form. Place the topping in the refrigerator until ready to use.

3. In a large mixing bowl, whisk together the superfine rice flour, potato starch, sorghum flour, baking powder, baking soda, and xanthan gum.

4. In the bowl of a stand mixer, cream together the sugar and shortening until they are light and fluffy. Scrape down the sides of the bowl and beat in the applesauce.

5. Add the dry ingredients and the cultured coconut milk in three alternating additions. Mix until the ingredients are evenly incorporated. Pour half of the batter into the loaf pan. Top with the diced apple and half of the streusel mix. Pour the remaining batter on top, smooth with a knife, and sprinkle with the remaining streusel.

6. Bake the cake for 35–40 minutes or until a toothpick inserted in the center comes out clean. Remove the cake from the oven to cool completely in the loaf pan before serving.

7. Tightly wrapped leftovers may be stored in the baking pan at room temperature for three days.

Note: The batter for this cake is very thick. Do not be alarmed if it seems thicker than regular cake batter.

Boston Cream Pie

Did you know that Jell-O vanilla pudding (the cook-and-serve variety) is dairy-free? I didn't know either until recently. I whip this up using the cooked Jell-O vanilla pudding as a quick filling. This Boston cream pie is so rich and delicious, but I still can't figure out why it's called pie. Use a little of the pudding to fill the cake, and pour the leftovers into small serving bowls for a snack later on. **Serves 10–12**

1. Empty the pudding package into a medium saucepan, pour in the coconut milk, and cook the pudding according to the directions on the box. Pour the filling into a large, heatproof container and refrigerate until the pudding is completely cooled.

2. Preheat the oven to 350°F and lightly grease two 8-inch round cake pans.

3. Prepare the Basic Vanilla Cake according to the recipe instructions and pour the batter into the prepared pans. Bake for 30–35 minutes or until golden and a toothpick inserted in the center comes out clean. Let the cakes cool in the pans for 15 minutes and then turn them out onto a wire rack to cool completely before filling and frosting.

4. While the cake and filling are cooling, make the Chocolate Glaze according to the recipe directions.

5. To construct the cake, place one layer of cake on a serving platter and spread it with $1/2$–$3/4$ cup of the pudding filling. (Reserve the remainder of the filling for another use.) It should be enough to generously cover the cake but not ooze out the sides. Place the second cake layer atop the pudding filling. Spread the top of the cake with the Chocolate Glaze. It is fine to let the glaze run down the sides of the cake. Serve immediately.

6. Leftovers may be covered and refrigerated for three to five days.

1 package Jell-O vanilla cook-and-serve pudding
2 cups coconut milk (see Where to Shop, p. 182)
1 recipe Basic Vanilla Cake (p. 134)
1 recipe Chocolate Glaze (p. 151)

Candy Bar Pie

When I was little, my brother asked for an ice cream pie every year for his birthday. I asked my mom how she made these pies and she responded, "Oh you know, just some ice cream in a graham cracker crust." What?! It was that easy? Well, I originally intended to make this pie into a grasshopper pie, which you can still do by using chocolate cookies in the crust and peppermint ice cream in the filling, but I couldn't find the right ice cream. Standing in the freezer section, I saw chocolate ice cream. For some reason my thoughts turned to summertime at the pool and how much I used to like a frozen Snickers bar as a snack. I had to beg for those, but every once in a while I was lucky enough to score one. And then it came to me . . . my brother's favorite ice cream pie plus my favorite Snickers bar equals a brand new favorite: Candy Bar Pie! **SERVES 10–12**

For the Crust

1 (8.3-ounce) box Enjoy Life Foods Crunchy Vanilla Honey Graham Cookies

7 tablespoons refined liquid coconut oil

1 tablespoon plus 1 teaspoon agave nectar

For the Filling

2 pints dairy- and soy-free chocolate ice cream (see Where to Shop, p. 182)

6 tablespoons warm Soft Salted Caramel (p. 178)

2 tablespoons SunButter or homemade sunflower seed butter (see Where to Shop, p. 182)

1–2 tablespoons chocolate syrup for drizzling (see Where to Shop, p. 182)

1. Place the cookies, coconut oil, and agave nectar in the bowl of a food processor. Pulse them together until the cookies are finely ground crumbs. The mixture will look very wet. Dump the mixture into the bottom of a 9-inch pie plate and press it onto the bottom and sides to form a crust. Place the crust in the refrigerator to chill for at least an hour.

2. When the crust has chilled, remove the ice cream from the freezer to soften for about 15–20 minutes; if it is very hot out, it will not need as much time to soften.

3. While the ice cream is softening, if the Soft Salted Caramel has been prepared ahead and refrigerated, place it in a microwave-safe bowl and microwave it on high for 10 seconds or until it is soft and spreadable. Pour and spread the sauce into the bottom of the prepared crust until it covers the entire bottom of the crust.

4. Spread the SunButter on top of the caramel sauce.

5. Spoon the ice cream in the pie pan over the SunButter and spread it with a knife or spatula until it is smooth and meets the sides of the crust.

6. Return the pie to the freezer for an hour to set. Drizzle with the chocolate syrup just before serving.

Caramel Kiss Cookies

I remember spending the weekend with a friend in high school, and her mother made a version of these cookies with peanut butter cups. I was enchanted. It never occurred to me that one could press a peanut butter cup into the center of a cookie and end up with something so tasty. So when I developed my Caramel Cups recipe (p. 150), I wondered if I could do the same thing with a caramel cup. These gluten-, dairy-, soy-, nut-, and egg-free cookies are delightfully delicious, and there is not one trace of peanut in them. These are a special treat that my girls beg for time and time again. They are an occasional holiday treat because they do require a bit of work.

MAKES 22 COOKIES

1 recipe Caramel Cups (p. 150)
1 cup superfine rice flour
1/3 cup potato starch
2 tablespoons sorghum flour
1/4 teaspoon salt
1/2 teaspoon xanthan gum
1/2 teaspoon baking soda
1 tablespoon ground flaxseed meal
3 tablespoons water
1/2 cup organic palm fruit oil shortening (butter-flavored or plain)
1/3 cup plus 1 tablespoon light brown sugar
1/3 cup plus 1 tablespoon granulated sugar
1/2 teaspoon vanilla extract
Mini muffin tin

1. Prepare the Caramel Cups according to the recipe directions and keep them refrigerated until ready to use.

2. Preheat the oven to 350°F.

3. In a large mixing bowl, whisk together the superfine rice flour, potato starch, sorghum flour, salt, xanthan gum, and baking soda. Set them aside.

4. In a small bowl, mix together the ground flaxseed meal and the water and let them stand for about a minute to thicken.

5. In the bowl of a stand mixer, cream together the organic palm fruit oil shortening and the sugars until they are light and fluffy. Add the thickened flaxseed mixture and the vanilla extract to the batter and beat for 30 seconds. Scrape down the sides of the bowl. Very slowly, add in the dry ingredients and stir them with the mixer on the lowest setting to moisten. Turn the mixer up to medium and stir until the ingredients are thoroughly combined and no dry bits remain.

6. Scoop the dough out with a 1 tablespoon measuring spoon and roll it into balls. Place one ball of dough in each well of a mini muffin tin. Place the tin in the oven and bake the cookies for 8 minutes.

7. Remove the muffin tins from the oven and press one Caramel Cup into the center of each cookie until it is firmly nestled.

8. Return the muffin tin to the oven to bake for another 3 minutes. When the cookies are done, remove the muffin tin from the oven and let the cookies cool completely in the muffin tins before removing.

9. Leftover cookies may be stored in an airtight container at room temperature for up to five days.

Cherry Cobbler

Cobblers are one of my all-time favorite summer desserts, and cherry is my favorite. When I was testing this recipe, I found myself trying to describe a cobbler to a British friend. She said she knew what a cobbler was: It was a fruity dessert with oatmeal and brown sugar on top. I stopped her and launched into a diatribe on the difference between a crisp, a crumble, and a cobbler. Frankly, I had no idea that I had so much useless knowledge warehoused in my brain. But then I remembered why I love cobblers the most. Basically, they are a lazy man's answer to making a shortcake. Instead of baking them individually, splitting the cakes, and putting some strawberries in the center, a cobbler is all of the ingredients thrown together in one pan and baked. Perhaps that's where the name comes from: It's just a few ingredients cobbled together to form one really spectacular dessert. Serves 10–12

For the Filling

4 pounds frozen, pitted dark, sweet cherries
1 tablespoon cornstarch
$1/4$ cup granulated sugar

For the Topping

2 cups superfine rice flour
$2/3$ cup potato starch
$1/3$ cup sorghum flour
$2 1/2$ teaspoons xanthan gum
1 teaspoon salt
1 tablespoon baking powder
1 teaspoon baking soda
$1/3$ cup granulated sugar
$1/4$ cup unsweetened applesauce
2 cups cultured coconut milk (see Where to Shop p. 182)
1 tablespoon cider vinegar
$1/3$ cup canola oil
2 teaspoons vanilla extract

1. Preheat the oven to 400°F.

2. In a large bowl, toss together the cherries, cornstarch, and $1/4$ cup sugar. Set aside.

3. To make the topping, whisk together the superfine rice flour, potato starch, sorghum flour, xanthan gum, salt, baking powder, baking soda, and $1/3$ cup granulated sugar in another large bowl. In a separate small bowl, whisk together the applesauce, cultured coconut milk, cider vinegar, canola oil, and vanilla extract. Create a well in the dry ingredients and pour the liquid ingredient mixture into the well all at once. Stir to combine until there are no dry bits remaining.

4. Pour the cherry mixture into 12 ramekins and, using a $1/2$-cup ice cream scoop, drop the topping batter onto the cherries.

5. Bake the cobbler for 25–30 minutes or until the cherries are bubbly and the cobbler topping is golden brown. Let the cobbler cool almost completely before serving; the juices will thicken as it cools. Serve immediately.

6. Leftovers may be covered and refrigerated for up to three days.

Chocolate Birds' Nests

These are a great treat to make with your kids because they can be cooked in the microwave and don't take too much effort to put together. The addition of the colorful jelly beans makes them a terrific springtime snack. If you ever have to do a classroom project with your child's class, these would be a great idea. MAKES APPROXIMATELY 2 DOZEN

3 cups gluten-free cornflakes or gluten-free crisped rice cereal
1 (10-ounce) bag gluten-, dairy-, soy-, nut-, and egg-free chocolate chips
Assorted soy- and wheat-free jelly beans

1. Line two baking sheets with parchment, waxed paper, or 24 paper cupcake tin liners.

2. Melt the chocolate over low heat (or in the microwave) until it is two-thirds melted. Remove the chocolate from the heat and stir until it is smooth. Pour the chocolate over the cereal and toss with a spatula to coat the cereal completely.

3. Drop heaping tablespoons of the chocolate-and-cereal mixture onto the lined sheet or into the individual paper liners. Make an indentation in the center with your knuckle or thumb. Place the birds' nests in the refrigerator to chill for 30–60 minutes. Remove from fridge and fill with jelly beans. Ta-da, birds' nests!

Chocolate Chip Bundt Cake with Espresso Glaze

As every parent with school-age children knows, there are a lot of potluck dinners and bake sales for which you'll need a quick and easy recipe. Our bake sales generally happen first thing in the morning, so I like to bring slices of this cake to perk up the parents on their way to work.
SERVES 10–12

Cake

1 recipe Basic Vanilla Cake
   (p. 134)
1 cup gluten-, dairy-, soy-, nut-, and egg-free semisweet mini chocolate chips or chunks

Glaze

1 cup confectioners' sugar, sifted
2–3 tablespoons brewed coffee

1. Preheat the oven to 350°F and lightly grease a 9-inch bundt pan. Prepare the Basic Vanilla Cake according to the recipe directions and fold in the chocolate chips. Spread the batter in the prepared bundt pan. Bake the cake for 55–60 minutes or until a toothpick inserted in the center comes out clean.

2. Remove the cake from the oven, let it cool in the pan for 30 minutes, and then turn it out onto a wire rack to cool completely.

3. When the cake is cool, mix together the confectioners' sugar and 2 tablespoons coffee until the glaze is smooth and spreadable. If the glaze is thick, add additional coffee, $1/4$ teaspoon at a time, until it is the desired consistency.

4. Spoon the glaze over the cooled cake, let the glaze set for about 30 minutes, and serve.

5. Wrap leftovers tightly and store in an airtight container at room temperature for up to three days.

Caramel Cups

Does anyone else love Rolos? I'll bet that there are at least a couple of you out there. My Caramel Cups recipe is great because it's allergy-free and it's also made with semisweet dark chocolate. Yum, the perfect combination of salty-sweet caramel and bittersweet chocolate. All you need is chocolate, my Soft Salted Caramel recipe, and chocolate candy cup molds for a quick and easy treat. I like to use a pastry bag and a small, clean paintbrush to put the chocolate in the candy molds, but you can use a spoon and a knife if you prefer. **MAKES 22 CUPS**

1 (10-ounce) bag gluten-, dairy-, soy-, nut-, and egg-free mini chocolate chips
1/2 teaspoon canola oil
Pastry bag with #4 tip (optional)
Candy cup molds
Paintbrush (optional)
1/3 cup Soft Salted Caramel (p. 178)

1. Microwave the chocolate chips and the canola oil together in a microwave-proof bowl on high until they are two-thirds melted, about 1 minute and 20 seconds. Remove the bowl from the microwave and stir the chocolate until it is completely smooth. Let the chocolate sit for at least 5 minutes or until it is cool enough to handle.

2. Load the cooled chocolate into a pastry bag fitted with a #4 tip (or spoon it in if desired). Pipe a little of the chocolate into the bottom of each candy mold. Working quickly, use a clean paintbrush (or knife) to smooth out the chocolate in the bottom of the molds and to work it up the sides. The chocolate should be thin on the sides but not transparent. Place the molds in the refrigerator and let the chocolate harden, about 15 minutes.

3. When the molded chocolate has set, remove it from the refrigerator and fill each cup with 1/4 teaspoon Soft Salted Caramel.

4. Pipe chocolate on top of the caramel to fill the cup and then smooth out the top with a knife. Return the molds to the refrigerator to chill for another hour.

5. Gently remove the Caramel Cups from the molds and refrigerate in an airtight container for up to a week. Keep refrigerated until just before using.

Chocolate Glaze

This is rich and delicious and makes the perfect topping for little cakes. This chocolate glaze will be enough to make a glossy finish on top of your Cream-Filled Chocolate Cupcakes (p. 156) or your Chocolate Surprise Snack Cakes (p. 164), but feel free to double it if you'll need it to glaze a larger cake. MAKES 1½ CUPS

1. Combine all of the ingredients in the top of a double boiler set over medium heat. Bring the water to a simmer and stir the ingredients constantly until they are completely smooth, being careful that the chocolate does not scorch. Remove the mixture from the heat.

2. Let the glaze cool for 5 minutes before spreading it over cupcakes or other cakes.

2 cups gluten-, dairy-, soy-, nut-, and egg-free semisweet chocolate chips (about 1 10-ounce bag)

¼ cup Lyle's Golden Syrup

2 teaspoons canola oil

2 tablespoons coconut milk creamer (see Where to Shop, p. 182)

Chocolate Pretzel Pie

I feel like I could really just stop at the title with this one. Salty and sweet, rich and creamy with a crunchy crust, this is the epitome of icebox pie. When my husband and I first met and he found out that I liked to bake, he begged me to make what he called a "yogurt pie." I could never find a recipe for it, but I think it probably contained Cool Whip, yogurt, and Jell-O. This pretzel pie obviously is not fruity, but I think that it is a pretty close, chocolaty approximation according to my husband's descriptions and based on the number of slices that he's been known to eat. SERVES **10–12**

Crust

4 cups gluten-, dairy-, soy-, nut-, and egg-free pretzels (about 7 ounces)
7 tablespoons liquid coconut oil (I prefer refined for a neutral flavor)
3 tablespoons agave nectar

Filling

2³/₄ cups So Delicious coconut milk creamer, original flavor
1 (10-ounce) package gluten-, dairy-, soy-, nut-, and egg-free chocolate chips
8 ounces mini marshmallows

1. Place the pretzels in the bowl of a food processor. Pulse the pretzels until they are finely ground; they should yield 2 cups crumbs. Dump them into a 9-inch deep-dish pie plate. Add the coconut oil and agave nectar and stir until all of the crumbs are coated with oil and agave. Press the pretzel crumb mixture into the bottom and sides of the pie plate to form a crust. Place the crust in the refrigerator to chill for at least 3 hours.

2. Add the coconut milk creamer and chocolate chips to a large saucepan and heat them over medium heat, stirring constantly. Bring the creamer to a simmer and stir in the marshmallows until the mixture is completely smooth. Pour the chocolate-marshmallow mixture into the prepared crust. (There will be about 1¹/₂ cups filling left over and it makes a delicious pudding. Pour that into separate ramekins, chill until set, and serve as pudding if desired.)

3. Place the pie in the refrigerator and chill for at least 6 hours or until the filling is completely set. Serve immediately.

4. Leftovers may be tightly wrapped and refrigerated for up to three days.

Chocolate Pudding Parfaits

That sounds pretty fancy, doesn't it? Don't be fooled. I got this idea from that dessert that all of us either ate as kids or made with our kids—"dirt pudding." This is just a silky, rich, and creamy chocolate pudding layered with a sprinkle of smashed cookies and my Whipped Cream (p. 181). Please feel free to add gummi worms if you like. See, dessert that's easy as . . . pudding. **Serves 4**

1. Whisk together the cornstarch and sugar in a medium heavy-bottomed saucepan until they are thoroughly combined. Slowly whisk in the creamer until the mixture is smooth.

2. Place the saucepan on the stove over medium heat, stirring constantly, until the mixture begins to simmer. Stir in the chocolate chips. Continue cooking for another 5 minutes until the pudding comes to a boil and begins to thicken. Cook for another 30 seconds.

3. Remove the pudding from the heat and mix in the vanilla extract. Pour into a large heatproof bowl and press a sheet of plastic wrap directly on top of the pudding. Chill for 2 hours or until completely cool.

4. Place four wine glasses or parfait cups on the counter and fill each with 1/4 cup cooled pudding. Sprinkle the pudding with some of the crumbled cake and add Whipped Cream. Top with another 1/4 cup pudding and then add a generous dollop of Whipped Cream to finish. Continue on to the next cup and repeat until all four parfait cups are filled.

5. Serve immediately or chill the parfaits up to an hour before serving.

Note: You can also substitute leftover crumbled Plain Old Brownies (p. 168), Basic Vanilla Cake (p. 134) or crushed Enjoy Life Foods chocolate cookies for the unfilled snack cakes.

For the Pudding
1/4 cup cornstarch
1/2 cup sugar
2 cups So Delicious original flavor nondairy creamer
7 ounces gluten-, dairy-, soy-, nut-, and egg-free semisweet chocolate chips
1/2 teaspoon vanilla extract

For the Parfaits
2 or 3 unfilled Chocolate Surprise Snack Cakes (p. 164), crumbled
1 recipe Whipped Cream (p. 181)

Confetti Cupcakes

I have to tell you that there are few things that get my kids more excited than vanilla cupcakes with loads of frosting and rainbow sprinkles. So when the sprinkles ended up *inside* the cake, my girls were pretty much over the moon with excitement. I always let them stir in the sprinkles. They can never get over the fact that they will disappear and only leave a little burst of color behind. **MAKES 24 CUPCAKES**

1 recipe Basic Vanilla Cake (p. 134)

¼ cup gluten-, dairy-, soy-, nut-, and egg-free rainbow sprinkles, plus additional for decorating (see Where to Shop Guide, p. 182)

1 recipe Even Easier "Buttercream" Frosting (p. 162)

1. Preheat the oven to 350°F and line twenty-four cupcake tins with paper liners. Set them aside.

2. Prepare the Basic Vanilla Cake according to the recipe instructions. After the dry ingredients and cultured coconut milk have been mixed in, turn off the mixer and fold in the sprinkles with a spatula.

3. Fill the prepared cupcake tins about two-thirds full of batter and bake the cupcakes in the preheated oven for 22 minutes or until a toothpick inserted in the center comes out clean.

4. Let the cupcakes cool in the tins for 15 minutes and then turn them out onto a wire rack to cool completely before frosting.

5. Frost with the Even Easier "Buttercream" Frosting and top with the additional sprinkles, if desired.

6. Serve the cupcakes immediately or store at room temperature in an airtight container for up to three days. Completely cooled, unfrosted cupcakes may be frozen in airtight containers for up to three months.

Cream-Filled Chocolate Cupcakes

These were definitely one of my childhood favorites, and whenever I serve them to my kids and their friends, they fly right off the table. There is just something about that little surprise of yummy vanilla frosting in the center that gets them every time. MAKES 18 CUPCAKES

2 cups superfine rice flour
²/₃ cup potato starch
¹/₃ cup sorghum flour
1 teaspoon xanthan gum
2 cups sugar
6 tablespoons unsweetened
    cocoa powder
1¹/₂ teaspoons baking soda
2 teaspoons instant espresso
    powder (optional)
¹/₂ teaspoon salt
³/₄ cup canola oil
1¹/₂ teaspoons vanilla extract
1 tablespoon cider vinegar
2 cups hot water
1 recipe Even Easier
    "Buttercream" Frosting
    (p. 134)
Pastry bag with #4 or #5 tip
1 recipe Chocolate Glaze
    (p. 151)
2 cups sifted confectioners'
    sugar

1. Preheat the oven to 350°F and line eighteen cupcake tins with paper liners. Set aside.

2. In a large mixing bowl, whisk together the superfine rice flour, potato starch, sorghum flour, xanthan gum, sugar, unsweetened cocoa powder, baking soda, instant espresso powder, and salt.

3. In another bowl, whisk together the oil, vanilla extract, vinegar, and water. Make a well in the center of the dry ingredients, pour in the wet ingredients, and mix until they are thoroughly blended. Pour the batter into the prepared cupcake tins and bake in the preheated oven for 18–22 minutes or until a toothpick inserted in the center comes out clean.

4. Remove the cupcakes from the oven and let them cool for 10 minutes in the tins before removing to wire racks to cool completely.

5. While the cupcakes are cooling, load the prepared buttercream into a pastry bag fitted with a #4 or #5 tip.

6. Prepare the frosting by making the Chocolate Glaze according to the recipe and then beating in the confectioners' sugar until it reaches a spreadable consistency.

7. When the cupcakes are cool, insert the pastry tip into the cupcake about halfway in, and then inject a little of the buttercream. Spread the top with the chocolate glaze. Continue until all of the cupcakes are filled and frosted. Let the glaze set for about 10 minutes, and then use the leftover buttercream in the pastry bag to make the characteristic loopty-loop across the top.

8. Serve immediately or store leftovers in an airtight container at room temperature for up to three days.

Eggnog Ice Cream

Do you ever get tired of the same old ice cream flavors? There are plenty of options for people with food allergies these days, but sometimes I just want something completely out of the ordinary, so I make my own. This year So Delicious sent me some eggnog creamer, and since I drink coffee black and didn't want it to go to waste, I turned it into a brand new ice cream flavor. Man, is this delicious served atop my Pumpkin Pie with Gingersnap Crust (p. 170). It was perfect on Thanksgiving.

SERVES 4

3 cups cold So Delicious Vegan
   Coconut Milk Nog, divided
1 tablespoon cornstarch

1. Place $2^3/_4$ cups "eggnog" in a large saucepan and bring to a boil over medium-high heat. Meanwhile, in a small bowl, whisk together the remaining $1/_4$ cup eggnog and the cornstarch until they are smooth. When the eggnog begins to boil, whisk in the cornstarch mixture and, stirring constantly, continue to boil for 1 minute. Remove from the heat.

2. Pour the custard mixture into a heatproof bowl with plastic wrap pressed directly on top and place it in the refrigerator to cool completely.

3. Freeze the completely cooled custard in an ice cream machine according to manufacturer's directions.

4. Serve immediately (it melts quickly) or freeze in an airtight container for up to three months.

"Fried" Ice Cream

In Ohio we had a lot of Chi-Chi's restaurants around, and even though I never went to one because my parents don't like spicy food, I always drooled over the commercials. I was always intrigued by fried ice cream. Was it really fried? What made it magical enough to survive the fryer without melting? What was on top of it? Surely, it was all a ruse! Well, I grew up and finally tried fried ice cream, and now I know that it is true—ice cream can be fried. However, in order to do it, the ice cream needs to be dunked in batter that usually contains wheat and eggs to hold it all together. This is a problem for my immune system. So, when I was planning this book, I had to come up with a way around it, and this was the easy solution! This ice cream isn't fried, but the topping contains all of the elements and flavors of traditional fried ice cream. I took it one step further by using coconut-milk ice cream. The coconut flavor adds extra dimension when mixed with the cinnamon and the honey. I tip my sombrero to this crunchy, sweet treat. **MAKES 1¼ CUPS TOPPING, SERVES 6**

2½ cups gluten-free cornflake cereal

2 tablespoons brown sugar

2½ teaspoons ground cinnamon

3 pints vanilla coconut-milk ice cream

½ cup honey for drizzling

6 Maraschino cherries for topping (optional)

1. Combine the cornflakes, brown sugar, and ground cinnamon in the bowl of a food processor. Pulse until they form a coarse meal.

2. Scoop out ½-cup servings of ice cream and divide them among six small bowls. Sprinkle each serving of ice cream with 2 tablespoons topping, drizzle with 1 tablespoon honey, and top with a cherry, if desired. Serve immediately.

3. Any unused topping may be stored in an airtight container at room temperature for up to two weeks.

Even Easier "Buttercream" Frosting

Just because I create a recipe and put it in a cookbook or a blog post doesn't mean that I think that it's forever finished. There is no such thing as perfection; there is always room for improvement in my allergy-free frosting, which was the hardest thing that I made for my first book. Over the years, the introduction of newer, better ingredients has made making frosting easier. I think you'll agree that this one is not only rich and creamy but also a breeze to make. MAKES 2¾ CUPS FROSTING, OR ENOUGH TO FROST **24** CUPCAKES OR **1** DOUBLE-LAYER **8**-INCH CAKE

1 cup organic palm fruit oil shortening, butter-flavored or plain

1 tablespoon powdered vanilla rice milk

1 pound confectioners' sugar

¼ cup plus 1 tablespoon vanilla coconut milk creamer

1. Add the shortening to the bowl of a stand mixer and beat for 1 minute. Scrape down the sides and beat in the powdered rice milk.

2. Scrape down the sides again and slowly stir in the confectioners' sugar. The mixture will be crumbly.

3. With the mixer on the lowest setting, pour in the coconut milk creamer. Blend just until the sugar is moistened. Stop the mixer and scrape down the sides.

4. Turn the mixer to medium-high and beat for 1 minute. Use the frosting immediately.

5. Any unused frosting may be refrigerated in an airtight container for up to five days or frozen for up to three months. Let the frosting come to room temperature and stir vigorously for 1 minute before using.

Kitchen Sink Cookies

Don't worry, you don't make these in the kitchen sink. I was thinking more along the lines of "everything but the . . . " These are dense and moist and even passed the oops-I-forgot-to-put-these-in-an-airtight-container-overnight test. That means that they continued to stay dense and moist, not dry and crumbly, even though they were left out on the cooling rack for ten hours. In my opinion, that is the test of a really good cookie. The inspiration for this cookie came from a high school baking session with my roommate, Christy, and a teacher named Miss Finkelstein. Miss Finkelstein just kept adding ingredients and adding more ingredients. I'm surprised that the kitchen sink didn't end up in the cookies! **MAKES ABOUT 22 COOKIES**

1. Preheat the oven to 350°F and line two baking sheets with parchment paper. Set aside.

2. In a large mixing bowl, whisk together the gluten-free flour, xanthan gum, baking soda, baking powder, gluten-free oats, and cinnamon. Set aside.

3. In the bowl of a stand mixer, cream together the shortening and the sugars until they are light and fluffy. While they are creaming, mix together the flaxseed meal and the water in a separate bowl and let them stand for 1 minute. Stop the mixer and scrape down the sides of the bowl. Add the flaxseed mixture and the vanilla extract to the batter and beat it again for a minute. Stop the mixer and scrape down the sides again. Add in the dry ingredients and stir with the mixer on low speed until the batter is moistened. Turn the mixer up a little higher and mix until the ingredients are completely incorporated. Stop the mixer and fold in the cereal, coconut, chocolate chips, and raisins.

4. Drop the dough by rounded tablespoons onto the lined sheets, 2 inches apart, and press them down slightly with the bottom of a glass.

5. Bake the cookies for 12 minutes. Remove from the oven and let them cool on the sheets for 10 minutes. Then remove the cookies to wire racks to cool completely.

6. Serve immediately, or store in airtight containers at room temperature for up to three days. Completely cooled cookies may also be frozen in airtight containers for up to three months.

$1\frac{1}{4}$ cups Bob's Red Mill Gluten-Free All-Purpose Baking Flour

1 teaspoon xanthan gum

1 teaspoon baking soda

1 teaspoon baking powder

$2\frac{3}{4}$ cups certified gluten-free oats

$\frac{3}{4}$ teaspoon cinnamon

1 cup organic palm fruit oil shortening (butter-flavored or plain)

1 cup packed light brown sugar

$\frac{1}{2}$ cup granulated sugar

2 tablespoons ground flaxseed meal

6 tablespoons water

1 teaspoon vanilla extract

$\frac{1}{2}$ cup gluten- and soy-free crisped rice cereal

$\frac{1}{4}$ cup flaked, sweetened coconut (about $1\frac{1}{2}$ ounces)

$\frac{1}{2}$ cup gluten-, dairy-, soy-, nut-, and egg-free mini chocolate chips

$\frac{1}{2}$ cup raisins

Chocolate Surprise Snack Cakes

As a kid in Ohio, I had never heard of Drake's snack cakes until *The Rosie O'Donnell Show* came on the air. In our neck of the woods, it was Hostess or Little Debbie, and we always had both around the house. I loved Ho-Hos, my brother dug the Twinkie, and my mother was a die-hard Donut Sticks fan. Once I moved to New York, I got to see what all the fuss was about: Yodels, Devil Dogs, Funny Bones—they are in every deli. My husband is a Yodel eater and tortures me by eating them in the car. They smell so good—and I cannot have them! So I decided to make my own version. These chocolate snack cakes are so yummy, and now I pack them up and take them in the car. Of course, I'm nice and share. Sometimes. **Makes 16 Cakes**

For the Cakes

8 éclair pans
2 cups superfine rice flour
$2/3$ cup potato starch
$1/3$ cup sorghum flour
$1^1/2$ cups granulated sugar
6 tablespoons cocoa powder
2 teaspoons baking soda
1 teaspoon salt
1 teaspoon xanthan gum
2 cups cold water
$2/3$ cup canola oil
6 tablespoons cider or white vinegar
1 teaspoon vanilla

1. Preheat the oven to 325°F and lightly grease eight éclair pans. (See Where to Shop, p. 182.) Set aside.

2. In a large mixing bowl, whisk together the superfine rice flour, potato starch, sorghum flour, granulated sugar, cocoa powder, baking soda, salt, and xanthan gum.

3. In another bowl, whisk together the water, canola oil, vinegar, and vanilla.

4. Pour the liquid ingredients into the dry ingredients and stir well until the batter is smooth and no dry bits remain. Spoon the batter into the prepared éclair pans, filling each about two-thirds full. Bake the cakes for 18 minutes or until a toothpick inserted in the center comes out clean. Remove the cakes from the oven and let cool in the pans for 10 minutes. Run a knife around the edges and turn the cakes out onto a wire rack to cool completely before filling and glazing.

5. While the cakes are cooling, make the filling. Measure out the 1 $1/2$ cups of frosting and reserve the leftovers for another use. Stir together the buttercream frosting with the SunButter. When the SunButter is completely mixed in, spoon the filling into a pastry bag fitted with a #4 or a #6 tip. Set the filled pastry bag aside.

6. When the cakes are completely cool, fill them. Hold one in your hand with the flat side up. Insert the tip of the pastry bag into the cake, about ¼ inch from the end, about halfway in. Squeeze out a small amount of the frosting, pulling the pastry bag out of the cake as you squeeze so as not to overfill and crack the cake. Repeat in the center of the cake and, again, about a ¼-inch from the other end of the cake. Repeat until all of the cakes are filled in this manner.

7. When all of the cakes are filled, return them to a wire rack set over a piece of parchment paper. Place the cakes rounded side up and spoon the glaze over them, smoothing it with a knife if desired. Let the glaze set for about an hour and serve.

8. Leftovers may be stored in an airtight container at room temperature for up to three days.

Note: Éclair pans make the shape of these cakes just right, and they are great for making Twinkies, too! If you have trouble finding them in your area, the Norpro brand pans are available on Amazon.

Note: Reserve a couple of the unfilled, unfrosted cakes and freeze them for later use in the Chocolate Pudding Parfaits (p. 153).

Filling

1½ cups Even Easier "Buttercream" Frosting (p. 162)

2 tablespoons SunButter (see homemade version in Where to Shop, p. 186)

Pastry bag with #4 or #6 tip

1 recipe Chocolate Glaze (p. 151)

Gingersnaps

When I was little, my grandparents always had a little jar of spice drops out for us to eat, and these cookies taste just like the spice drops I remember. These are a pumped-up version of the cookie and contain anise as well as pieces of candied ginger. My friend—and chief taste tester—Maija swears that these are the best cookie I've ever made. I have to add that when these cookies were cooling in the kitchen, I caught my husband sneaking in there five different times to grab more. Clearly, they are a favorite. **Makes 22 cookies**

2 cups Bob's Red Mill Gluten-Free All-Purpose Baking Flour

1 teaspoon xanthan gum

1 tablespoon Chinese five-spice powder

1/2 teaspoon salt

1/2 teaspoon baking soda

3/4 cup plain organic palm fruit oil shortening (not butter-flavored)

1 cup sugar

1 tablespoon flaxseed meal

3 tablespoons water

1/4 cup molasses

1 (4-ounce) package candied ginger, finely chopped (see Where to Shop Guide, p. 182)

1. Preheat the oven to 325°F and line two baking sheets with parchment paper.

2. In a large mixing bowl, whisk together the all-purpose flour, xanthan gum, five-spice powder, salt, and baking soda. Set aside.

3. In the bowl of a stand mixer, cream together the shortening and sugar until it becomes light and fluffy. Scrape down the sides.

4. Mix together the flaxseed meal and the water in a separate bowl, let thicken for 1 minute, and add the mixture to the batter. Beat until the batter is light and fluffy again. Scrape down the sides of the bowl and add the molasses. Beat again. Scrape down the sides and stir in the dry ingredients until they are completely incorporated. Fold in the candied ginger.

5. Using a 1 1/2-inch ice cream scoop, transfer the dough to a baking sheet, leaving 1 1/2 inches between each cookie.

6. Bake for 12 minutes in the preheated oven until the edges are just golden and the centers are set.

7. Let the cookies cool for 10 minutes on the baking sheet and then remove them to wire racks to cool completely before serving.

8. Leftovers may be stored in an airtight container at room temperature for up to five days.

Plain Old Brownies

Honestly, sometimes you just need a good brownie: a rich, dense, fudgy, gooey, stick-to-the-top-of-your-mouth brownie. None of this cake-like brownie business. This is like a brick of chocolate fudge, and I mean it. I know that you have been looking for this recipe since you, or your child, were diagnosed because I have been, too. It took a while to get this one just right. The trick is taking the brownies out of the oven after twenty-two minutes so they stay moist and fudgy. I ran the bake sale at my oldest daughter's school one Thanksgiving, and I was surprised that the brownies sold better than the fancy cut-out cookies and all kinds of over-the-top cupcakes. I'm not sure why I was surprised; kids often know what the adults forget: Keep it simple. **MAKES 24 BROWNIES**

1 cup superfine rice flour

¼ cup potato starch

2 tablespoons sorghum flour

¾ cup plus 2 tablespoons cocoa powder

2 teaspoons baking powder

¾ teaspoon baking soda

1 teaspoon salt

1 teaspoon xanthan gum

1 cup organic palm fruit oil shortening, butter-flavored or plain

1¼ cups packed dark brown sugar

½ cup unsweetened applesauce

¼ cup dairy- and soy-free chocolate syrup (I use Ah!Laska)

2 teaspoons vanilla extract

1 (10-ounce) bag gluten-, dairy-, soy-, nut-, and egg-free Enjoy Life Foods Mega Chunks or mini chocolate chips

1. Preheat the oven to 350°F and lightly grease the bottom of a 9 x 13-inch glass baking dish. Set aside.

2. In a large bowl, whisk together the superfine rice flour, potato starch, sorghum flour, cocoa powder, baking powder, baking soda, salt, and xanthan gum. Set aside.

3. In the bowl of a stand mixer, cream together the shortening and brown sugar. Scrape down the sides of the bowl and beat in the applesauce and chocolate syrup. Scrape down the sides again and stir in the vanilla extract. Stir in the dry ingredients until they are completely incorporated.

4. Fold in the chocolate chips. Spread the batter in the prepared baking pan and smooth the top with a knife. Bake the brownies in the preheated oven for 22 minutes or until the top is set and the brownies spring back slightly when they are touched. Do not overbake.

5. Let the brownies cool completely before cutting.

6. Leftovers may be stored in an airtight container at room temperature up to five days.

Some Add-In Ideas

• Stir in 1 teaspoon peppermint extract with the vanilla to make these into Grasshopper Brownies.

• Stir in 1 teaspoon cinnamon and ½ teaspoon chipotle chile powder into the flour mixture to make these into Aztec Chocolate Brownies.

• Stir in 1 teaspoon orange extract and 1 tablespoon orange zest with the vanilla extract to make these into Chocolate Chip Orange Brownies.

Pumpkin Pie with Gingersnap Crust

Sometimes I just need a change of pace. I love pumpkin pie. It's really my favorite part of Thanksgiving, but eating the same pie year after year can become quite tiresome. Especially when it's been the same pie recipe for thirty-plus years. So this year I decided to create a different crust, and that made all the difference. The use of my Gingersnaps as a crust punched this pie up enough to make it taste so new and different that no one could believe it. Everyone clamored for seconds, which is, in my opinion, the hallmark of an instant classic. Serves **10–12**

Crust

Approximately 14 Gingersnaps
  (p. 166)
¼ cup butter-flavored organic
  palm fruit oil shortening,
  melted

Filling

2 cups pureed pumpkin
½ cup light brown sugar
½ cup granulated sugar
1½ teaspoons cinnamon
¼ teaspoon nutmeg
½ teaspoon salt
1 cup So Delicious plain
  coconut milk creamer
¼ cup plus 2 tablespoons
  cornstarch

1. Preheat the oven to 325°F.

2. Pulse the Gingersnaps in the bowl of a food processor until they become small crumbs. Measure out 2 cups, pour the crumbs into a mixing bowl, add the melted shortening, and mix well to coat. Dump the crumbs into a 9-inch deep-dish pie plate and press them in to form a crust. (I like to use the back of a metal spoon for this.) Place the crust in the preheated oven and bake for 5 minutes. Remove the crust from the oven and let it cool completely.

3. Turn the oven up to 350°F.

4. In another large mixing bowl, whisk together the pureed pumpkin, the light brown sugar, granulated sugar, cinnamon, nutmeg, and salt.

5. In a smaller, separate bowl, whisk together the coconut milk creamer and cornstarch until they are smooth. Stir the coconut milk mixture into the pumpkin mixture until it forms a smooth custard, and then pour it into the cooled crust.

6. Bake the pie in the preheated oven for 75 minutes or until the custard is set in the center. If the edges of the pie begin to burn, cover them with aluminum foil.

7. Carefully remove the pie from the oven and let it cool completely. After the pie is completely cool, place it in the refrigerator to set up overnight.

8. Leftovers may be covered and refrigerated for up to five days.

Rhubarb Compote

Perhaps you'll cook this one up when rhubarb is first available in May and serve it over Shortcakes (p. 176) with a generous portion of Whipped Cream (p. 181) on top. Perhaps you'll decide to just store it in an airtight jar and use it in place of jam on toast or a Waffle (p. 54). Or, what about spooning some of it onto some dairy-free ice cream? Yum. It doesn't really matter how you use it, because whichever way you choose is most definitely the right way. My friend Lucy always has a big batch of this cooking on her stove in the weeks just before Memorial Day. Happy memories. SERVES **6**

4 cups diced rhubarb
1 ⅓ cups plus 1 tablespoon sugar
1 teaspoon lemon juice

1. Add all of the ingredients to a saucepan fitted with a lid and stir to combine. Heat the mixture over medium heat, stirring frequently until the rhubarb begins to soften and the sugar dissolves.

2. Cover the pan and continue cooking for 7–10 minutes or until the mixture thickens and the rhubarb is tender. Remove the pot from the heat and transfer the compote to a heatproof container to cool completely before serving.

3. Leftovers may be refrigerated in an airtight container for up to five days.

Rocky Road Cookies

No peanuts? No problem. My girls adore marshmallows, and I love chocolate. When I think of the two together, I think of either s'mores or rocky road ice cream. The other day I was trying to come up with a new treat for the cookie jar, and I decided to give rocky road cookies a whirl. The saltiness of the sunflower seeds perfectly offsets the sweetness of the chocolate, marshmallows, and chocolate chips. I love how these are a little crispy at the edges and soft in the center.
MAKES ABOUT 22 COOKIES

1½ cups Bob's Red Mill Gluten-Free All-Purpose Baking Flour

⅔ cup cocoa powder

1 teaspoon baking soda

1 teaspoon baking powder

1 teaspoon salt

1 teaspoon xanthan gum

1 cup organic palm fruit oil shortening (butter-flavored or plain)

¾ cup light brown sugar

2 tablespoons flaxseed meal

6 tablespoons water

1 teaspoon vanilla

¾ cup gluten-, dairy-, soy-, nut-, and egg-free Enjoy Life Foods mini chocolate chips

¼ cup roasted sunflower seeds, salted or unsalted

½ cup mini marshmallows

1. Preheat the oven to 350°F and line two baking sheets with parchment paper. Set them aside.

2. In a large mixing bowl, whisk together the all-purpose flour, cocoa powder, baking soda, baking powder, salt, and xanthan gum until they are thoroughly combined. Set aside.

3. In the bowl of a stand mixer, beat together the organic palm fruit oil shortening and the brown sugar until they are light and fluffy. Scrape down the sides of the bowl.

4. In a small separate bowl, mix together the flaxseed meal and the water and let them stand for 1 minute to thicken. Add the flaxseed mix and vanilla extract to the batter and beat again for another 30 seconds. Scrape down the sides and then slowly add the dry ingredients. Stir until the dry ingredients are thoroughly incorporated. Fold in the chocolate chips, sunflower seeds, and marshmallows.

5. Drop by tablespoonfuls onto the prepared baking sheets. Bake in the preheated oven for 12 minutes. Remove the cookies from the oven and let them cool on the sheets for 10 minutes before transferring them to wire racks to cool completely.

6. Serve immediately or store the cooled cookies in airtight containers at room temperature for up to three days. Alternately, the completely cooled cookies may be frozen in an airtight container for up to three months.

Shortcakes

I didn't want to brand these as strawberry, peach, or blueberry because shortcake is so versatile that you can serve it with any kind of fruit or preserves that you have on hand. I particularly like these with my Rhubarb Compote (p. 172) and a generous dollop of my Whipped Cream (p. 181). They are tender and flaky like biscuits—a modern take on old-fashioned shortcakes!

MAKES 8 SHORTCAKES

2 cups superfine rice flour

$^2/_3$ cup potato starch

$^1/_3$ cup sorghum flour

$2^5/_8$ teaspoons xanthan gum

1 tablespoon baking powder

1 teaspoon baking soda

2 tablespoons granulated
   sugar

1 cup cultured coconut milk
   (see Where to Shop, p. 182)

1 cup water

$^1/_3$ cup canola oil

$^1/_4$ cup unsweetened
   applesauce

1. Preheat the oven to 400°F.

2. In a large mixing bowl, whisk together the rice flour, potato starch, sorghum flour, xanthan gum, baking powder, baking soda, and sugar.

3. In another bowl, whisk together the cultured coconut milk, water, canola oil, and applesauce. Pour the liquid mixture into the dry ingredients all at once and stir until they are thoroughly combined and no dry bits remain.

4. Using a $^1/_2$-cup ice cream scoop, scoop out the dough, and place the ball on an unlined and ungreased baking sheet. You can flatten it very slightly if you like. Repeat with the remaining dough and bake the shortcakes in the preheated oven for 20 minutes or until they are golden and cooked through. Serve immediately.

Soft Salted Caramel

If caramel is one of your favorite candies, but you cannot have dairy, then I'll bet it has been awhile since you've had it. Well, get ready, because I give you dairy- and soy-free caramel! This is a soft caramel that works well as a filling in my Caramel Cups (p. 150) or slightly warmed as a sauce in the bottom of Candy Bar Pie (p. 140). You can definitely eat it by the spoonful, too. Keep this caramel refrigerated when you aren't using it. Microwave about ¼ cup for 10 seconds so that it is spoonable or spreadable. Just make sure that you use a candy thermometer and really keep your eye on it while you are cooking this. Otherwise you'll end up with toffee, which is tasty, too, but not what we are trying to make! **MAKES 2 CUPS**

Canola oil
Candy thermometer
½ cup dairy- and soy-free margarine (see Where to Shop, p. 182)
½ pound packed light brown sugar
¾ cup plus 1 tablespoon Sweetened Condensed Milk (p. 180)
½ cup Lyle's Golden Syrup or light corn syrup
¼ teaspoon salt
½ teaspoon vanilla extract

1. Lightly coat the inside of a small metal bowl with a little canola oil and set it aside.

2. Combine all of the ingredients minus the vanilla extract in a large, heavy-bottomed saucepan and bring them to a boil over medium-high heat, stirring constantly. When the mixture begins to boil, insert a candy thermometer and cook the mixture until it reaches 240°F (soft ball stage). Continue cooking for 2 minutes or until the mixture reaches 248°F, being careful that the temperature does not rise above this.

3. Remove the caramel from the heat and carefully stir in the vanilla extract; be careful because it may splatter when it is added to the hot caramel. Pour the mixture into the prepared bowl and let it cool at room temperature until you are ready to use.

4. When the caramel is cool, if it is not in use, it should remain refrigerated in an air-tight container for up to one week. Let it warm to room temperature before using.

Note: Sugar temperatures rise very quickly toward the end of the cooking time. Be sure to keep a very close eye on the temperature of your caramel.

Note: This is not a recipe to make with children. Boiling sugar can cause very serious burns.

Magic Squares

As a kid, I loved Eagle Brand Magic Cookie Bars, and I don't know many people from my generation who don't. We had these at almost every school, birthday, and church bazaar when I was growing up, and I think that the flaked coconut on top is what began my love affair with coconut in general. But without dairy, wheat, eggs, nuts, or soy, I thought that the magic was gone. These were forever off my list of things to eat. Now I know that, indeed, where there's a will, there's a way. And it's a yummy one. Make these bite-size for your tea party or a little bigger if you are making them to satisfy a sweets craving. **Makes 24 squares**

1. Preheat the oven to 350°F and lightly grease a 9 x 13-inch baking pan.

2. Prepare the Sweetened Condensed Milk according to the recipe directions. Set aside.

3. In a separate bowl, whisk together the rice flour, potato starch, sorghum flour, baking soda, baking powder, xanthan gum, salt, and cinnamon.

4. In the bowl of a stand mixer, cream together the organic palm fruit oil shortening and brown sugar until they are fluffy. Scrape down the sides and beat in the honey.

5. Mix together the flaxseed meal and the water in a separate bowl and add this mixture to the batter. Beat the batter until it is light and fluffy again. Scrape down the sides.

6. Slowly stir in the dry ingredients and mix until the dough comes together and all the ingredients are evenly incorporated.

7. Press the dough into the prepared baking dish and bake for 10 minutes in the preheated oven.

8. Pour the Sweetened Condensed Milk over the crust and scatter the chocolate chips, marshmallows, and flaked coconut on top. Return the pan to the oven and bake for another 22 minutes or until the Sweetened Condensed Milk is set and the coconut and marshmallows are just golden. Remove from the oven. Allow to cool completely before cutting into squares.

9. Serve immediately. Store leftovers for up to three days in an airtight container at room temperature.

1 recipe Sweetened Condensed Milk (p. 180)
1½ cups superfine rice flour
½ cup potato starch
¼ cup sorghum flour
1 teaspoon baking soda
1 teaspoon baking powder
1 teaspoon xanthan gum
1 teaspoon salt
¾ teaspoon cinnamon
1 cup organic palm fruit oil shortening, butter-flavored or plain
1¼ cups packed light brown sugar
¼ cup honey
2 tablespoons ground flaxseed meal
6 tablespoons water
¾ cup mini gluten-, dairy-, soy-, nut-, and egg-free chocolate chips
1½ cups mini marshmallows
1⅓ cups flaked, sweetened coconut

Sweetened Condensed Milk

A vital component to so many old recipes, I knew I needed to develop a gluten-, dairy-, soy-, and nut-free sweetened condensed milk recipe. Since I came up with this one, I have been able to make so many new goodies such as my Soft Salted Caramel (p. 178) and Magic Squares (p. 179). I have yet to just dump it over a little fruit (as I loved to do when I was a girl), but I'm sure I'll try that next! MAKES 1¼ CUP

3 tablespoons dairy- and soy-free margarine (see Where to Shop, p. 182)

²/₃ cup granulated sugar

1 cup Better Than Milk Vanilla Vegan Rice Powder

1¼ cups boiling water

1. Melt the margarine in a saucepan and stir in the sugar and the powdered vanilla rice milk. Remove the mixture from the heat and stir in the boiling water.

2. Return the saucepan to the heat and cook over medium heat, stirring constantly, until the mixture is smooth and has thickened. Use immediately.

Whipped Cream

Could it be? Whipped cream?! Yes it could, and it is so easy that you will not believe it. I love whipped cream, and though I have found dairy-free brands at the supermarket and health food store, it can get pricey and is sometimes hard to find. I like to make my own. The key to making this whipped cream is that the ingredients, the bowl, and the beaters should be refrigerated until the minute you are ready to start, and make sure that you do not shake the coconut milk or you will not be able to skim the cream off the top. Whip this up and drop a generous dollop on berries.
SERVES 4

1. Place a large metal mixing bowl, the metal beaters from a hand-held mixer, and the cans of coconut milk in the refrigerator for at least 2 hours.

2. Remove the cans from the refrigerator, open, and skim the solid cream off the top of each can of coconut milk. *If the cream is not solid but still soft, return it to the refrigerator to chill until it is solid; otherwise this recipe will not work.* This should yield about 2 cups solid coconut cream. Discard the remaining coconut water or reserve for another use.

3. Place the coconut solids in the bottom of a chilled metal bowl, add the vanilla extract, and beat on medium speed for about 30 seconds or until the coconut solids are creamy and soft peaks form. Use immediately or refrigerate, uncovered, for up to an hour. The whipped cream will soften considerably at room temperature.

2 (14-ounce) cans coconut milk, unshaken and refrigerated
1 teaspoon vanilla extract

Where to Shop

Please note that brands can change their manufacturing practices and ingredients at any time without warning. *Always* check the ingredients label and allergy statement closely before buying any new ingredients.

Apple Butter—I like the Vermont Organics brand of apple butter because the spice blend is nice and there is no added sugar. However, you may use any brand you like. I buy Vermont Organics at my local health food store, Whole Foods, and online at www.bestofvermont.com.

Bacon—I am a huge fan of Applegate farms bacon and sausage. Lately I have been seeing it at more and more chain supermarkets like IGA and Shop Rite as well as at Whole Foods. If you cannot find it in your neighborhood, check their website for vendors: www.applegatefarms.com.

Beef Stock—I always make my own chicken stock but rarely make beef stock. Try More Than Gourmet's Ready to Use Beef Stock. It is gluten-, dairy-, soy-, nut-, and egg-free. I buy it in my local bodega, but it is also available directly from More Than Gourmet (www.morethangourmet.com) and in chain supermarkets nationwide.

Bob's Red Mill Gluten-Free All-Purpose Baking Flour—What a long way we have come since I was diagnosed with food allergies! Bob's complete line is available in most supermarkets nationwide. If you can't find it in your local shop, try buying it online at Amazon or directly from Bob's at www.bobsredmill.com.

Bow-Tie Pasta, Gluten-Free—My Kasha and Pasta recipe (p. 102) is based on the traditional kasha *varnishkes,* which is made with bow-tie pasta. I generally use whatever small, gluten-free pasta I have on hand, but if you can't bear making it without bow-ties, try La Veneziane brand. I have only ever seen it online. It is available from Gluten Free Palace: www.glutenfreepalace.com/Le-Veneziane.

Canned Salmon—Unfortunately, we live in a time where we have to be very careful about BPA in our cans and plastic. I buy all of my canned fish from Vital Choice (www.vitalchoice.com). Though a little more expensive, I feel that the safety and quality of the fish is worth it.

Canned Sweet Potato Puree—I like to roast my own sweet potatoes if I'm making my Salmon Croquettes (p. 34), but if you are rushed, used organic canned sweet potatoes. I like Farmer's Market brand and get them at Whole Foods or the health food store in my neighborhood. I usually find them in the canned vegetable section next to the pumpkin puree.

Chicken Stock—I like to use my recipe from *The Complete Allergy-Free Comfort Foods Cookbook* for homemade chicken stock, but if you are short on time, I like Imagine brand chicken stock. It is available in most chain supermarkets nationwide.

Chile de Árbol—I usually find *chile de árbol* at Whole Foods or in our local Latin market. If you cannot find it near you, you can definitely order it online from www.thelatinproducts.com.

Chinese Rice Sticks—These refer to the "glass noodles" that are available in many national supermarket chains. Look in the international section for the Ka-Me brand, though there are others that are equally good. Always check the label for possible cross-contaminants.

Chocolate Chips and Chocolate Chunks—I only buy Enjoy Life Foods dairy-, soy-, nut-, and egg-free Mini Chips and Mega Chunks. I also like their Boom Choco Boom chocolate bars. They make all of their products in a dedicated gluten-free facility and do not use soy lecithin as an emulsifier. I have found their products in Kroger, Meijer, Shop Rite, Whole Foods, and also online at Amazon.

Chocolate Syrup—I love the Ah!Laska brand, which is available at Whole Foods and other natural food stores nationwide. Nesquik is also dairy- and soy-free and available at almost every supermarket in the United States.

Corn Flour—Corn flour is available at most supermarkets nationwide. Maseca and Bob's Red Mill are my favorite brands.

Crystallized Ginger—I am a big fan of the organic, crystallized ginger from The Ginger People, and I buy it at Whole Foods. Find vendors in your neighborhood on their website's store locator: www.gingerpeople.com/storelocator/location/map.

Cultured Coconut Milk—This used to be called coconut milk kefir, but the name has changed. I buy the So Delicious brand and find it in the refrigerated dairy section of most supermarkets as well as in health food stores. If you cannot find it in your neighborhood, check their website to find vendors (www.sodelicious.com) or ask your local market to order it for you.

Dairy-Free Ice Cream—I use chocolate So Delicious coconut-milk ice cream in my Candy Bar Pie (p. 140) because it is dairy- and soy-free and tastes great. I buy it at Whole Foods.

Dairy- and Soy-Free Margarine—I prefer Earth Balance dairy- and soy-free margarine spread and buy it at chain supermarkets like King Kullen, Kroger, Shop Rite, and Whole Foods. It is also available online at Amazon.

Éclair Pans—These obviously aren't an ingredient, but you may be scratching your head about what they are. Éclair pans are available at most housewares stores. Do not choose a set that is labeled ladyfinger pans—they are too shallow. I prefer the Norpro brand (available at Amazon) because they are deeper and, I think, make the final presentation nicer.

Gluten-Free Crisped Rice Cereal—I always buy the Erewhon brand gluten-free crisped rice cereal, and I find it at the health food store, Whole Foods, and sometimes at national chains like Kroger. Do not confuse this with puffed rice cereal. It is not the same. Also, always read the label. Erewhon makes a gluten-free variety as well as one made with malt, which is not gluten-free.

Gluten-Free Graham Cookies—Enjoy Life Foods Crunchy Vanilla Honey Graham Cookies are my favorite for making cookie crusts. They are available at Whole Foods and health food stores, and you can also check the website (www.enjoylifefoods.com) for vendors. They will even give you a printable request letter that you can give to your local grocery store if you can't find their products in your neck of the woods!

Jelly Beans—I always use Jelly Belly jelly beans because they are gluten-, dairy-, soy-, nut-, and egg-free. Jelly Belly beans are available nationwide at most supermarkets, candy stores, and drug stores.

Kielbasa—There is a lot of junk, like MSG, in some sausages that is not safe for delicate immune systems. I recommend Wellshire Farms or Coleman Natural Sausages. I find both at Whole Foods. For a list of vendors in your area, consult their websites: www.wellshirefarms.com, www.colemannatural.com.

Kosher Gelatin—Kosher gelatin substitute is really easy to find in New York City. Most of our supermarkets carry it in their kosher section. However, if you have trouble tracking it down, try ordering it online from www.allinkosher .com. For vegan gelatin, look for agar-agar flakes in your supermarket's international section.

Lundberg Roasted Brown Rice Couscous—This is an excellent substitute for quinoa or millet and is available at most Whole Foods, Jungle Jim's, and health food stores nationwide.

Mustard—My heart belongs to Maille for its flavor. Watch out for additives like soy in the form of xanthan not grown on corn in some mustard brands. If I cannot find Maille at the supermarket, then I also like Bournier. Shop Rite nationwide stocks Maille, and both are generally available at the regular supermarket in the condiment section.

Organic Palm Fruit Oil Shortening—Spectrum brand is the easiest brand to find in supermarkets, but if you are concerned about cross-contamination, I also like Tropical Traditions organic palm fruit oil shortening, which is available online at www.tropicaltraditions.com. Jungle Jim's and Whole Foods also carry their own brands of organic palm fruit oil shortenings. They are usually marked as "all-vegetable shortening." A quick check of the ingredients reveals palm fruit oil. This shortening is sometimes in the oils section of the supermarket and at other times in the baking-needs section.

Peppermint Candies—I use Bob's candy canes but not their starlight mints for Bark So Many Ways (p. 132). At the time of publication, the starlight mints were made on shared equipment with nuts. The candy canes are not. Bob's candy canes are available online at Amazon and at www.oldtimecandy.com as well as in supermarkets nationwide.

Powdered Vanilla Rice Milk—There are two brands that I recommend: Growing Naturals (www.growingnaturals.com) and Better Than Milk (www.btm soymilk.com) brands. Both are available directly from the manufacturers and also on Amazon.

Pretzels, Soy-Free—This one was hard to track down, but I recommend the Ener-G gluten-free Wylde pretzels to make the crust for my Chocolate Pretzel Pie (p. 152) because they are also soy-free. They are available in health food stores and also directly from Ener-G at www.ener-g.com/wylde-pretzels.html.

Raw Coconut Aminos—This is such a great replacement for soy sauce. I buy the Coconut Secret brand at Jubilee market, but if you do not have a Jubilee in your area, check your local supermarket and health food store before ordering it from Amazon.

Soba Noodles—Eden Organic is my most trusted brand for 100 percent buckwheat soba noodles. I buy them at Whole Foods or at my health food store but have also seen them at chain supermarkets nationwide. Usually they are in the international section with the sushi ingredients.

Sprinkles—For my Confetti Cupcakes (p. 154), I used Hanna's Gourmet Candy Sprinkles for the batter and topping. However, if you are concerned about cross-contamination, you could use colored sanding sugar or sprinkles made by India Tree. They do not process nuts in the facility and use only vegetable ingredients. You could also use Sprinklz brand, which is available at Whole Foods. They are gluten-, dairy-, soy-, nut-, and egg-free.

SunButter—I love SunButter because it is not only peanut-free but it is made in a dedicated peanut-free facility. It can be found nationwide at most supermarket chains or on Amazon. However, if you are concerned about possible soy cross-contamination, try making your own by grinding 2 cups sunflower seeds with a little canola oil in the food processor until the mixture is smooth like SunButter. This could take 10–15 minutes in the processor, but be patient. It works!

Superfine Rice Flour or Chinese Rice Flour—This rice flour is ground so fine that you will never make a gritty cake or cookie again. I love to buy the superfine sweet white rice flour from Authentic Foods and usually get it on Amazon. However, superfine rice flour can also be found in Asian markets.

Tostadas—If I'm having trouble finding soy-free tostada shells, I often just make my own (see the recipe notes, p. 6). If you do not feel like getting out your fryer, Charras Natural Baked Tostadas have no added oil or soy and can be ordered online from the Latin Products at www.thelatinproducts.com.

Vanilla Extract—There are so many great brands of vanilla extract now. My favorite is Frontier brand, and I buy it at my local health food store or at Whole Foods.

Vegan White Chocolate—If you can tolerate soy lecithin, try Vegan Sweets dairy-free white chocolate chips. I get them at Amazon.

Xanthan Gum, Soy-Free—I buy Ener-G soy-free xanthan gum directly from the company, online at www.ener-g.com.

Acknowledgments

There are so many people that I would like to thank for helping me with this book. I could go on for pages and pages, but that would just be too much. First, thank you to my wonderful and loving husband, Jesse, who loaned me his precious props for the photo shoot and broke his diet to taste every recipe in the book. Tamar Rydzinski and Lara Asher—oh how I love working with both of you! I could not think of a better, more supportive team, and I feel so fortunate to have found you both. Thank you for always believing in me and encouraging me when I feel like I just cannot think of one more recipe. You always know that I can even when I think I can't. Melani Bauman and Lorna Palmer: This book is gorgeous, and I knew it would be from the minute we did our first photo shoot together all those years ago. Your work is extraordinary, and I hope that you know it. Thank you for making it a piece of art. To Carmen, thank you for being so patient with my extreme messiness and for putting up with the bomb explosion that is my kitchen when I'm developing new recipes. I could not do this without you. Margot and Colombe, I know that the time I spend working is time that I am not with you, and I am grateful to both of you for letting me explore this career. Maija and Steve, thank you for never saying no to food and for the offer to loan out some freezer space. I rely heavily upon your critiques. Shahla Zarraby, thank you for taking the time to talk to me about Persian cooking, and for teaching me about rose petals in food and the Persian way of cooking rice. I used to crave your food in high school, and now I can make it at home. Dorthea Casselman, thank you, again, for helping me with the math necessary for these recipes and for never, ever—even when I was fourteen years old—laughing at my math inabilities. Thank you to my mom and dad and Ann for letting me experiment in the kitchen from the earliest days and for cleaning up after me. Thank you to Samantha Mandor, Cory Bishop, and Temptu for making me look so good in the photos! Thank you also to Courtenay Smith, Carla Levy, Brettne Bloom, Rachel Spielman, and all of my other friends who have provided either professional or emotional encouragement and support along the way. It has been invaluable. Finally, my books absolutely would not be possible without my fans who buy them. It is to you that I am most grateful. You inspire me and teach me new things every day. Thank you.

Recipe Index

About the Author

Elizabeth Gordon is the owner of the online gluten-, dairy-, soy-, nut-, and egg-free bakery Betsy & Claude Baking Co. She is the author of *The Complete Allergy-Free Comfort Foods Cookbook* and *Allergy-Free Desserts.* She writes a blog, *Allergy-Free Delights,* about parenting, baking, and her observation that the two are, in her life, inextricably intertwined. She trained in cake decorating under Toba Garrett at the Institute for Culinary Education and later interned for Elisa Strauss of Confetti Cakes in New York City. Diagnosed with egg and wheat allergies in 2003, Gordon left a social work PhD program at Fordham University to pursue the culinary arts. After she noticed that simply inhaling wheat particles in the kitchen and handling fondant and gum paste containing egg whites aggravated her condition, she began experimenting with alternative flours and egg substitutes, rather than giving up on a lifelong dream of baking professionally. Later, she combined these findings with her cake-decorating expertise to create beautiful and delicious hypoallergenic treats. She has an MSW from New York University, was an eating disorder therapist, and is a certified personal trainer as well as a full-time mother. She lives in New York City with her husband and two daughters. For more information and additional recipes, go to Elizabeth's website, www.myallergyfreelifestyle.com, or her blog, www.allergyfreedelights.com.